STUDY (

MW01519313

INDIANA CHRISTIAN UNIVERSITY

CHRISTIAN

FOUNDATIONS

*For no one can lay any foundation other than
the one already laid, which is Jesus Christ.*

I Corinthians 3:11

by
Dr. Lester Sumrall

Sumrall Publishing
P.O. Box 12
South Bend, IN 46624

PLEASE NOTE:
This study guide is designed to be a companion to the audio/video teaching tape, *Christian Foundations*, by Dr. Lester Sumrall.

It is a college workbook with space allowed for your personal notes.

All scriptures, unless otherwise indicated, are taken from the *King James Version of the Holy Bible*.

Audio and videotapes are available from Sumrall Publishing.

Copyright © All Rights Reserved
Reprinted December, 2001

CHRISTIAN FOUNDATIONS
ISBN No. 0-937580-74-0

Printed by Sumrall Publishing
P.O. Box 12
South Bend, Indiana 46624

www.sumrallpublishing.com

STUDY GUIDE

INDIANA CHRISTIAN UNIVERSITY

CHRISTIAN FOUNDATIONS

TABLE OF CONTENTS

STUDY GUIDE

INDIANA CHRISTIAN UNIVERSITY

CHRISTIAN FOUNDATIONS

Lesson 1

THE TRIUNE NATURE OF THE UNIVERSE

INTRODUCTION:

Everything in the universe, bearing the marks of perfection, is divinely engraved with a three. Man is positioned in a total universe of:

A.   Tripods--three extremities (not four or two)

B.   Triads--three things or ideas

C.   Triune--three in one

D.   Tripartite--three fold, three parities

E.   Tritheism--three distinct gods

F.   Trinity--three persons, or group of three

READING:

Romans 1:20, *For the invisible things of him from the creation of the world are clearly seen, being understood by the things that are made, even his eternal power and Godhead; so that they are without excuse.*

1.   TIME

We count the fullness of time by three:

A.   The past--old time

B.   The future--new time

C.   The present--uniting of time. The present holds hands with the past and the future; the livable part of time.

5

2.   SPACE

Total calculation of space is three:

A.   Longitude--length

B.   Latitude--breadth

C.   Altitude--height

3.   MATTER

Water, H_2O is three.

A.   Water is made up of three atoms:

1)   Two hydrogen

2)   One oxygen

B.   Water has three physical phases.

1)   Water is a liquid to drink.

2)   Water is a solid called ice.

3)   It can be a vapor called steam.

4.   A COMMON TREE IN YOUR YARD

These three make a whole.

A.   It is bark.

B.   It is pulp.

C.   It is sap.

To remove one is to destroy all.

5. THE ATOM IS MADE UP OF THREE

   A.   Proton--the positive charge

   B.   Electron--the negative charge

   C.   Neutron--uncommitted

There can be no universe without all three, living and flowing together. Each is an important part of the whole.

6. THE SPIRIT, SOUL, AND BODY OF MAN IN RELATION TO TRAVEL

   A.   Man first traveled in his lowest form, the body.

      1)   On foot

      2)   By animal

   B.   Later, man traveled by the inventions of his soul. He traveled by boat, wagon, car, etc. It was soulical. It was earthbound.

   C.   Today, modern man has the potential to travel by his spirit.

      1)   In the air

      2)   To outer space

      3)   To the throne of God (visions)

7. SATAN APPEALED TO EVE THROUGH THE THREE PARTS OF HER BEING

   A.   Genesis 3:1, *Now the serpent was more subtil than any beast of the field which the LORD God had made. And he said unto the woman, Yea, hath God said, Ye shall not eat of every tree of the garden?*

   This was Satan's appeal to the body of Eve, to her appetite.

B.   Genesis 3:4, *And the serpent said unto the woman, Ye shall not surely die.*

This was an appeal to the soul of Eve: to her reason, her thinking, her will power.

C.   Genesis 3:5, *For God doth know that in the day ye eat thereof, then your eyes shall be opened, and ye shall be as gods, knowing good and evil.*

This was Satan's appeal to her spirit: her conscience or intuition, her relationship with God.

8.   EVE RESPONDED TO SATAN BY BODY, SOUL, AND SPIRIT

A.   Genesis 3:6, *And when the woman saw that the tree was good for food...*

The physical part of Eve, her appetite, surrendered to Satan.

B.   Genesis 3:6, *. . .that it was pleasant to the eyes. . .*

The eyes are windows to the soul. Her mind had reasoned the matter. Her emotions had accepted it. Her will made her determined to eat.

C.   Genesis 3:6, *. . .and a tree to be desired to make one wise. . .*

This was a strike at her spirit to compete with God. From this we see that Eve fell three ways: by her spirit, soul and body.

9.   THREE KINDS OF LIGHT IN THE TABERNACLE

A.   The sun lit the Outer Court; the body is open to the elements.

B.   The Holy Place was lit by the lampstand; the soul is lighted by the mind, emotions and will.

C.   The Holy of Holies was lit by the Shekinah presence of God; the spirit of man is enlightened by the Spirit of God.

10. PETER AND THE FISH WITH A COIN

A.   Spirit: Jesus had the revelation of a certain fish with a coin in its mouth (Matthew 17:27).

B. Soul: Peter accepted His instructions and went to the water with line, hook and bait. His mind, emotions and will were involved.

C. Body: Peter's body obeyed. He caught the physical fish with the material coin in its mouth.

11. THE TRINITY OF SALVATION

A. All salvation from the beginning is in three parts.

I John 5:8, *And there are three that bear witness in earth, the Spirit, and the water, and the blood: and these three agree in one.*

B. Israel was saved from Egypt by:

1) The blood of the lamb on the door post

2) The dividing of the Red Sea

3) The cloud of glory which overshadowed them

Here we have the blood, the water, and the Spirit.

12. THE GIFTS OF THE SPIRIT

The very heart of the church is made up of three plus three plus three, which means perfection plus perfection plus perfection, or nine gifts of the Spirit.

I Corinthians 12:8-10, *For to one is given by the Spirit the word of wisdom; to another the word of knowledge by the same Spirit;*
v. 9, *To another faith by the same Spirit; to another the gifts of healing by the same Spirit;*
v. 10, *To another the working of miracles; to another prophecy; to another discerning of spirits; to another divers kinds of tongues; to another the interpretation of tongues.*

13. THERE ARE ALSO NINE FRUIT OF THE SPIRIT

A. The nine fruit of the Spirit reveal the perfection of three plus three plus three: Love, joy, peace, long-suffering, gentleness, goodness, faith, meekness and temperance.

Galatians 5:22-23, *But the fruit of the Spirit is love, joy, peace, longsuffering, gentleness, goodness, faith,*
v. 23, *Meekness, temperance: against such there is no law.*

B. The fruit of the Spirit divides itself into three equal categories.

1) First three (love, joy, and peace) are our relationship with God and are directed toward Him.

2) The next three (long-suffering, gentleness, and goodness) form our relationship with our fellow human beings.

3) The last three (faith, meekness, and temperance) determine our relationship with ourselves. They are directed toward our inner man.

14. THERE ARE NINE MINISTRIES OF AND TO THE CHURCH

A. The nine ministry gifts are: apostles, prophets, pastors, evangelists, teachers, elders or bishops, deacons, helps, and governments. They are men and women given by Christ to the church to minister.

I Corinthians 12:28, *And God hath set some in the church, first apostles, secondarily prophets, thirdly teachers, after that miracles, then gifts of healings, helps, governments, diversities of tongues.*

B. There are three purposes.

Ephesians 4:12, *For the perfecting of the saints, for the work of the ministry, for the edifying of the body of Christ.*

1) The perfecting of the saints

2) The work of the ministry

3) The edifying of the Body of Christ

This is truly a remarkable record of the number three.

15. DAY OF PENTECOST

A. Body

Acts 2:1, *. . . they were all with one accord in one place.*

B. Soul--They were obedient by an act of will to the Lord, who had told them to wait in Jerusalem.

Luke 24:49, *And, behold, I send the promise of my Father upon you: but tarry ye in the city of Jerusalem, until ye be endued with power from on high.*

C.   Spirit--They had a visitation of the Holy Spirit.

Acts 2:4, *And they were all filled with the Holy Ghost, and began to speak with other tongues, as the Spirit gave them utterance.*

16.   THREE FEASTS OF ISRAEL

A.   Unleavened Bread, or Passover

Exodus 23:15, *Thou shalt keep the feast of unleavened bread: (thou shalt eat unleavened bread seven days, as I commanded thee, in the time appointed of the month Abib; for in it thou camest out from Egypt: and none shall appear before me empty:)*

B.   Firstfruits, or Pentecost

Exodus 23:16, *And the feast of harvest, the firstfruits of thy labours, which thou hast sown in the field...*

C.   Ingathering, or Tabernacles

Exodus 23:16, *. . . and the feast of ingathering, which is in the end of the year, when thou hast gathered in thy labours out of the field.*

17.   THREE DESIRES OF GOD

III John 2, *Beloved, I wish above all things that thou mayest prosper and be in health, even as thy soul prospereth.*

A.   Prosper (spirit)

B.   Be in health (body)

C.   Soul to prosper (soul)

18.   THE MINISTRY OF JESUS

Luke 4:18, *The Spirit of the Lord is upon me, because he hath anointed me to preach the gospel to the poor; he hath sent me to heal the brokenhearted, to preach deliverance to the captives, and recovering of sight to the blind, to set at liberty them that are bruised.*

A.   Preach the gospel to the poor (spirit).

B.   Heal the brokenhearted and bring deliverance to the captives (soul).

C.   Bring recovery of sight to the blind and set at liberty those that are bruised (body).

19.   THE TEMPTATION OF JESUS

A.   Make stone become bread (body).

Matthew 4:3, *And when the tempter came to him, he said, If thou be the Son of God, command that these stones be made bread.*

B.   Jump from the Temple (soul).

Matthew 4:6, *And saith unto him, If thou be the Son of God, cast thyself down: for it is written, He shall give his angels charge concerning thee: and in their hands they shall bear thee up, lest at any time thou dash thy foot against a stone.*

C.   Bow to Satan (spirit).

Matthew 4:9, *And saith unto him, All these things will I give thee, if thou wilt fall down and worship me.*

20.   THREE STEPS TO SALVATION

Acts 2:38-39, *Then Peter said unto them, Repent, and be baptized every one of you in the name of Jesus Christ for the remission of sins, and ye shall receive the gift of the Holy Ghost.*
v. 39, *For the promise is unto you, and to your children, and to all that are afar off, even as many as the Lord our God shall call.*

A.   Repent (soul).

B.   Be baptized for the remission of sins (body).

C.   Receive the gift of the Holy Spirit (spirit).

STUDY GUIDE

INDIANA CHRISTIAN UNIVERSITY –

CHRISTIAN FOUNDATIONS

Lesson 2

THE TRIUNE NATURE OF
THE FATHER

INTRODUCTION:

Man is made in the image and likeness of God. He is a true image. The inner man, or spirit, is in the image of God, and the outer man, the body, is in the image of God.

John 1:18, *. . .No man hath seen (horao) God at any time. . .,* means that no one fully understood God at any time. The Greek word, *horao*, means to comprehend or understand. Christ declared, or interpreted, God to mankind (Dake Bible, p. 93).

READING:

Genesis 1:26-27, *And God said, Let us make man in our image, after our likeness: and let them have dominion over the fish of the sea, and over the fowl of the air, and over the cattle, and over all the earth, and over every creeping thing that creepeth upon the earth.* v. 27, *So God created man in his own image, in the image of God created he him; male and female created he them.*

1.   THE SPIRIT OF GOD THE FATHER

    A.   God is a spirit. He has a personal spirit.

       John 4:24, *God is a Spirit: and they that worship him must worship him in spirit and in truth.*

    B.   God's Spirit in creation

       Genesis 1:2, *. . .the Spirit of God moved upon the face of the waters.*

C. God's Spirit in redemption

Romans 8:15-16, *For ye have not received the spirit of bondage again to fear; but ye have received the Spirit of adoption, whereby we cry, Abba, Father.*
v. 16, *The Spirit itself beareth witness with our spirit, that we are the children of God.*

D. God's Spirit in revelation

Ezekiel 11:5, *And the spirit of the LORD fell upon me, and said unto me, Speak; Thus saith the LORD; Thus have ye said, O house of Israel: for I know the things that come into your mind, every one of them.*

God's Spirit reveals the future.

E. God's Spirit in communication

Revelation 2:7, *He that hath an ear, let him hear what the Spirit saith unto the churches; To him that overcometh will I give to eat of the tree of life, which is in the midst of the paradise of God.*

2. THE SOUL OF GOD THE FATHER

A. Divinity, perfection--never tainted with sin or clouded by doubt

B. His mind--greater than human comprehension. He created all things.

C. His emotions--anger, joy, etc.

D. His will--making decisions and determinations

3. THE BODY OF GOD THE FATHER

A. His body is about the same size as that of Jesus.

1) They stood together. Stephen saw Jesus standing beside God the Father.

Acts 7:55, 57, *. . . he, being full of the Holy Ghost, looked up stedfastly into heaven, and saw the glory of God, and Jesus standing on the right hand of God.*

v. 57, *Then they cried out with a loud voice, and stopped their ears, and ran upon him with one accord.*

        2)   The prophet Amos saw the Lord standing.

              Amos 9:1, *I saw the Lord standing upon the altar. . .*

B.   God has hands.

      Genesis 2:7, *And the LORD God formed man of the dust of the ground . . .*

C.   God has a face.

        1)   Genesis 32:30, *And Jacob called the name of the place Peniel: for I have seen God face to face . . .*

        2)   Exodus 33:11, *And the LORD spake unto Moses face to face, as a man speaketh unto his friend . . .*

D.   God has fingers.

        1)   Daniel 5:5, *In the same hour came forth fingers of a man's hand, and wrote over against the candlestick upon the plaster of the wall of the king's palace: and the king saw the part of the hand that wrote.*

        2)   Exodus 31:18, *And he gave unto Moses, when he had made an end of communing with him upon mount Sinai, two tables of testimony, tables of stone, written with the finger of God.*

E.   God has feet.

        1)   He walked with Adam.

              Genesis 3:8, *And they heard the voice of the LORD God walking in the garden in the cool of the day: and Adam and his wife hid themselves from the presence of the LORD God amongst the trees of the garden.*

        2)   He walked with Enoch.

              Genesis 5:22-24, *And Enoch walked with God after he begat Methuselah three hundred years, and begat sons and daughters:*
              v. 23, *And all the days of Enoch were three hundred sixty and five years:*
              v. 24, *And Enoch walked with God: and he was not; for God took him.*

F.   God has a voice.

   1)   He spoke at the baptism of Jesus.

        Matthew 3:17, *And lo a voice from heaven, saying, This is my beloved Son, in whom I am well pleased.*

   2)   He talked to Isaiah.

        Isaiah 1:2, *Hear, O heavens, and give ear, O earth: for the LORD hath spoken . . .*

G.   God has hinder parts.

     Exodus 33:23, *And I will take away mine hand, and thou shalt see my back parts: but my face shall not be seen.*

H.   God has a mouth. He ate with Abraham.

     Genesis 18:3-8, *And said, My Lord, if now I have found favour in thy sight, pass not away, I pray thee, from thy servant:*
     v. 4, *Let a little water, I pray you, be fetched, and wash your feet, and rest yourselves under the tree:*
     v. 5, *And I will fetch a morsel of bread, and comfort ye your hearts; after that ye shall pass on: for therefore are ye come to your servant. And they said, So do, as thou hast said.*
     v. 6, *And Abraham hastened into the tent unto Sarah, and said, Make ready quickly three measures of fine meal, knead it, and make cakes upon the hearth.*
     v. 7, *And Abraham ran unto the herd, and fetched a calf tender and good, and gave it unto a young man; and he hasted to dress it.*
     v. 8, *And he took butter, and milk, and the calf which he had dressed, and set it before them; and he stood by them under the tree, and they did eat.*

I.   God has ears.

   1)   Exodus 3:7, *And the LORD said, I have surely seen the affliction of my people which are in Egypt, and have heard their cry by reason of their taskmasters; for I know their sorrows.*

   2)   Isaiah 59:1, *Behold, the LORD's hand is not shortened, that it cannot save; neither his ear heavy, that it cannot hear.*

   3)   II Samuel 22:7, *In my distress I called upon the LORD, and cried to my God: and he did hear my voice out of his temple, and my cry did enter into his ears.*

16

J.   God has eyes.

   1)   Psalm 11:4, *The LORD is in his holy temple, the LORD's throne is in heaven: his eyes behold, his eyelids try, the children of men.*

   2)   Psalm 18:24, *Therefore hath the LORD recompensed me according to my righteousness, according to the cleanness of my hands in his eyesight.*

   3)   Psalm 33:18, *Behold, the eye of the LORD is upon them that fear him, upon them that hope in his mercy.*

NOTES

STUDY GUIDE

INDIANA CHRISTIAN UNIVERSITY

CHRISTIAN FOUNDATIONS

Lesson 3

THE TRIUNE NATURE
OF CHRIST

INTRODUCTION:

Death, which came to this earth because of sin, permeated man's spirit, soul, and body. Because of this, man must receive God's power in all three areas (His salvation is triune, or tripartite), spirit, soul, and body.

The man who sins must die. He must pay the penalty of judgment in three areas. In Luke 16, the man in hell was conscious of such judgment.

However, Jesus Christ was without sin in His spirit, soul and body. He suffered the penalty of sin for mankind to redeem him to God (John 3:16).

Our spirit, soul, and body have been judged in the sinless sacrifice of Christ. His death was accepted as our death. We have already died in the Lord.

READING:

Romans 5:18-19, *Therefore as by the offence of one judgment came upon all men to condemnation; even so by the righteousness of one the free gift came upon all men unto justification of life.*
v. 19, *For as by one man's disobedience many were made sinners, so by the obedience of one shall many be made righteous.*

Romans 8:1, *There is therefore now no condemnation to them which are in Christ Jesus, who walk not after the flesh, but after the Spirit.*

1. IN CHRIST WE SEE AN EXAMPLE OF DIVINE PERFECTION OF THE HUMAN PERSONALITY

A. Spirit

    1) Christ was born of the Spirit.

       Matthew 1:18, *Now the birth of Jesus Christ was on this wise: When as his mother Mary was espoused to Joseph, before they came together, she was found with child of the Holy Ghost.*

    2) When Christ was 12 years old He was guided and motivated by the Spirit, asking and answering questions in Jerusalem before the religious doctors. He did not learn these truths, they were revealed.

    3) Christ was anointed of the Spirit.

       Acts 10:38, *How God anointed Jesus of Nazareth with the Holy Ghost and with power: who went about doing good, and healing all that were oppressed of the devil; for God was with him.*

    4) The Holy Spirit rested upon Christ at baptism.

       Matthew 3:16, *And Jesus, when he was baptized, went up straightway out of the water: and, lo, the heavens were opened unto him, and he saw the Spirit of God descending like a dove, and lighting upon him.*

    5) Christ lived and ministered by the Spirit-freely, openly and joyfully.

       Matthew 4:23, *And Jesus went about all Galilee, teaching in their synagogues, and preaching the gospel of the kingdom, and healing all manner of sickness and all manner of disease among the people.*

    6) Christ's total body and soul were always subject to His spirit.

B. Soul

    1) His mind

       Philippians 2:5, *Let this mind be in you, which was also in Christ Jesus.*

      2)   His emotions--Jesus wept over Lazarus.

          John 11:34-36, *And said, Where have ye laid him? They said unto him, Lord, come and see.*
          v. 35, *Jesus wept.*
          v. 36, *Then said the Jews, Behold how he loved him.*

      3)   His will

          Luke 22:42, *. . .not my will, but thine be done.*

   C.   Body

      1)   His seeing--tender, kind, clean, and pure

      2)   His taste--under divine control

      3)   His feelings--aware of human need

      4)   His hearing--human tragedy

      5)   His speaking--words of truth, courage, love, and hope

2.   JESUS WORSHIPPED GOD THE FATHER BY HIS SPIRIT

   A.   By fasting

   B.   By vigils of prayer

   C.   By reading the Word in the synagogue

   D.   By witnessing

   E.   By ministering life, hope, joy, and healing

3.   JESUS LIVED BY HIS SPIRIT

   A.   He overthrew the moneychangers in the temple.

   B.   He spoke against hypocrisy.

   C.   He refused to be selfish or soulish.

   D.   He practiced forgiving and forgetting.

        Luke 23:34, *. . .Father forgive them. . .*

4. CHRIST REJECTED RELIGION DICTATED BY THE SOUL

A. He ignored the washing of hands by the Pharisees.

B. He refused the worship of days, such as the man-made laws about sabbaths.

C. He would not conform to the wearing of special clothes for religion.

5. CHRIST KNEW PEOPLE BY THE SPIRIT

A. The woman who gave a coin

B. The woman who washed His feet with tears

C. Changed Peter's name

D. Nathanael--a man without guile

6. AT TEMPTATION: CHRIST WON IN THREE WORLDS; EVE LOST IN THREE WORLDS

A. Satan asked Him to turn a stone to bread. Christ refused to make bread for Himself to eat (body).

B. The devil took Christ to the pinnacle of the Temple and challenged Him to jump as the angels would bear Him up. This would have been a display of pride (soul).

C. The devil showed Him all the nations of the world and said, "Worship me." Christ rebuked him (spirit).

7. THE THREE WORLD SUFFERINGS OF CHRIST

Christ suffered sin's most bitter pain in three dimensions. He suffered in His spirit, soul and body.

A. Physical suffering--the stripes, the thorns, the cross, the nails, the spear, and the slaps. He had no bed. He often hungered.

7/17/18

The Triune Nature of Christ
Lesson 3

> B. Soul suffering--the organ of self-consciousness. He bore the shame of the cross.
>
>> 1) Hebrews 12:2, *. . .who for the joy that was set before him endured the cross. . .*
>>
>> 2) John 12:27, *Now is my soul troubled. . .*
>>
>> 3) He had no clothes while on the cross. The laughing mob made sport of Him.
>>
>> Matthew 26:38, *. . .My soul is exceeding sorrowful, even unto death. . .*
>>
>>> a) Judas betrayed Him.
>>>
>>> b) Peter cursed, and then denied Him.
>>>
>>> c) The rest ran and hid in fear.
>
> C. Spirit suffering
>
>> 1) He craved for fellowship, yet was alone.
>>
>> 2) He desired companionship, yet was deserted.
>>
>> 3) He suffered spiritual separation.
>>
>> Matthew 27:46, *. . .My God, my God, why hast thou forsaken me?*

NOTES

_____

_____

_____

_____

_____

_____

_____

_____

_____

_____

_____

_____

_____

_____

_____

_____

_____

_____

_____

_____

_____

_____

_____

_____

STUDY GUIDE

INDIANA CHRISTIAN UNIVERSITY

CHRISTIAN FOUNDATIONS

Lesson 4

THE TRIUNE NATURE OF THE HOLY SPIRIT

INTRODUCTION:

The Holy Spirit is the third member of the Trinity. He has a personality and a will all His own even though He is intimately united with the Father and the Son.

READING:

John 14:16-17, *And I will pray the Father, and he shall give you another Comforter, that he may abide with you for ever;*
v. 17, *Even the Spirit of truth; whom the world cannot receive, because it seeth him not, neither knoweth him: but ye know him; for he dwelleth with you, and shall be in you.*

1.   THE HOLY SPIRIT IS DIVINE

    A.   He is continually referred to in the Scripture as the Spirit of the Lord, or the Spirit of God, denoting His divinity.

        1)   Luke 4:18, *The Spirit of the Lord is upon me, because he hath anointed me to preach the gospel to the poor; he hath sent me to heal the brokenhearted, to preach deliverance to the captives, and recovering of sight to the blind, to set at liberty them that are bruised.*

        2)   I Corinthians 6:11, *And such were some of you: but ye are washed, but ye are sanctified, but ye are justified in the name of the Lord Jesus, and by the Spirit of our God.*

        3)   II Corinthians 3:17, *Now the Lord is that Spirit: and where the Spirit of the Lord is, there is liberty.*

B.   He has divine attributes.

    1)   Omnipresent

        Psalm 139:7, *Whither shall I go from thy spirit? or whither shall I flee from thy presence?*

    2)   Omniscient

        I Corinthians 2:10, *But God hath revealed them unto us by his Spirit: for the Spirit searcheth all things, yea, the deep things of God.*

    3)   Omnipotent

        a)   Luke 1:35, *And the angel answered and said unto her, The Holy Ghost shall come upon thee, and the power of the Highest shall overshadow thee: therefore also that holy thing which shall be born of thee shall be called the Son of God.*

        b)   Romans 15:19, *Through mighty signs and wonders, by the power of the Spirit of God; so that from Jerusalem, and round about unto Illyricum, I have fully preached the gospel of Christ.*

    4)   Eternal

        Hebrews 9:14, *How much more shall the blood of Christ, who through the eternal Spirit offered himself without spot to God, purge your conscience from dead works to serve the living God?*

2.   THE HOLY SPIRIT IS A SPIRIT BEING

A.   His very name reveals this truth.

B.   He communicates with God, the function of the spirit.

    I Corinthians 2:10, *But God hath revealed them unto us by his Spirit: for the Spirit searcheth all things, yea, the deep things of God.*

3.   THE HOLY SPIRIT HAS A SOULICAL NATURE

A.   He has a will, part of the soulical realm.

    I Corinthians 12:11, *But all these worketh that one and the selfsame Spirit, dividing to every man severally as he will.*

B.   He has emotions, part of the soulical realm.

1)   He can be grieved.

Ephesians 4:30, *And grieve not the holy Spirit of God, whereby ye are sealed unto the day of redemption.*

2)   He manifests love.

II Timothy 1:7, *For God hath not given us the spirit of fear; but of power, and of love, and of a sound mind.*

3)   He groans.

Romans 8:26, *Likewise the Spirit also helpeth our infirmities: for we know not what we should pray for as we ought: but the Spirit itself maketh intercession for us with groanings which cannot be uttered.*

C.   He has a mind, also part of the soulical realm.

Romans 8:27, *And he that searcheth the hearts knoweth what is the mind of the Spirit, because he maketh intercession for the saints according to the will of God.*

4.   THE HOLY SPIRIT CAN MANIFEST HIMSELF IN BODILY FORM

Matthew 3:16, *And Jesus, when he was baptized, went up straightway out of the water: and, lo, the heavens were opened unto him, and he saw the Spirit of God descending like a dove, and lighting upon him.*

5.   THE WORK OF THE HOLY SPIRIT

A.   He is a teacher.

John 14:26, *But the Comforter, which is the Holy Ghost, whom the Father will send in my name, he shall teach you all things, and bring all things to your remembrance, whatsoever I have said unto you.*

B.   He is a comforter.

John 14:16, *And I will pray the Father, and he shall give you another Comforter, that he may abide with you for ever.*

C.   He is an empowerer.

Acts 1:8, *But ye shall receive power, after that the Holy Ghost is come upon you: and ye shall be witnesses unto me both in Jerusalem, and in all Judæa, and in Samaria, and unto the uttermost part of the earth.*

D.   He gives gifts to men.

I Corinthians 12:8-10, *For to one is given by the Spirit the word of wisdom; to another the word of knowledge by the same Spirit;*
v. 9, *To another faith by the same Spirit; to another the gifts of healing by the same Spirit;*
v. 10, *To another the working of miracles; to another prophecy; to another discerning of spirits; to another divers kinds of tongues; to another the interpretation of tongues.*

E.   He gives fruit to men.

Galatians 5:22-23, *But the fruit of the Spirit is love, joy, peace, longsuffering, gentleness, goodness, faith,*
v. 23, *Meekness, temperance: against such there is no law.*

F.   He keeps men from sin.

Galatians 5:16, *This I say then, Walk in the Spirit, and ye shall not fulfil the lust of the flesh.*

G.   He reproves the world.

John 16:8, *And when he is come, he will reprove the world of sin, and of righteousness, and of judgment.*

H.   He helps Christians pray.

Romans 8:26, *Likewise the Spirit also helpeth our infirmities: for we know not what we should pray for as we ought: but the Spirit itself maketh intercession for us with groanings which cannot be uttered.*

I.   He helps Christians praise.

I Corinthians 14:15, *What is it then? I will pray with the spirit, and I will pray with the understanding also: I will sing with the spirit, and I will sing with the understanding also.*

STUDY GUIDE

INDIANA CHRISTIAN UNIVERSITY

CHRISTIAN FOUNDATIONS

Lesson 5

THE TRIUNE NATURE
OF MAN

INTRODUCTION:

Man himself was created a triune being.

READING:

I Thessalonians 5:23, *And the very God of peace sanctify you wholly; and I pray God your whole spirit and soul and body be preserved blameless unto the coming of our Lord Jesus Christ.*

1. MAN IS A TRINITY

    A. Hebrews 4:12-13, *For the word of God is quick, and powerful, and sharper than any two-edged sword, piercing even to the dividing asunder of soul and spirit, and of the joints and marrow, and is a discerner of the thoughts and intents of the heart.*
        v. 13, *Neither is there any creature that is not manifest in his sight: but all things are naked and opened unto the eyes of him with whom we have to do.*

    B. The personality of man is so closely knit that it takes the all-powerful Word of God to even divide the soul from the spirit. This is true in action and definition.

    C. Philosophy and psychology do not have the answers to the reality of soul and spirit.

2. THE BODY

A. Almighty God fashioned a human body from the clay of the earth.

Genesis 2:7, *And the LORD God formed man of the dust of the ground, and breathed into his nostrils the breath of life; and man became a living soul.*

There is a close kinship between man and his environment. His outer shell is like the area in which he lives.

B. The body is easy to classify and identify. The five senses with which it relates to the world are: seeing, feeling, smelling, tasting, and hearing.

C. We shall see that this earthly part of man was created to be a slave to the immortal part of man, his spirit. If the inward man is evil, the carnal, clay man will manifest this evil.

D. If the inner man is spiritual, the physical man demonstrates the fruit of the spirit.

3. THE SOUL

A. Inside man's shell, or clay house, God placed a soul. This part of man is his real self, having a close relationship with his outer shell, or body. This soul is made up of three tremendous areas:

1) Intellect--man thinks
2) Emotions--man feels
3) Willpower--man decides

B. God joined the body and soul together by His breath. God created these first two areas to be subservient to the third area. Man's body and soul can be good or bad in relationship to the third area.

4. THE SPIRIT

A. Inside the clay house, behind his soul, or his thinking, feeling, and will, God placed man's spirit. This spirit is as distinct from the other two areas of man as darkness is from light. God gave man's spirit the propensity of communion with deity. In this area, he would be able to communicate with the divine world. God gave man, in his spirit, the structure of intuition and the power of conscience. By this, man would feel what was right and what was wrong; what was good or bad, spiritually and morally.

B. There was a perfect blending and harmonizing of the three distinct elements of spirit, soul, and body in creating the human and his personality.

This is what we mean when we say that man is made up of three parts which should function as one whole. Thus, man was created a trinity.

5. THE PERFECT MAN

A. With his body, he walks, eats, sees, hears and feels with his five God-given senses. This is what we see.

B. With his soul, the man Adam possessed the power to name all of the animals on the earth. With it he had the intellect to operate the Garden of Eden as its overseer. He possessed emotions to admire the sunrise and the sunset, and to feel affection toward his wife, Eve. He had the willpower to choose what he would do as he walked in the Garden as its king.

C. With his spirit, man walked with God in the evening time and conversed with Him. With his spirit, he understood his limitations such as eating the forbidden fruit from the Tree of Knowledge of Good and Evil.

6. KING, SERVANT, AND SLAVE

A. God made man's spirit to be the king of this trinity.

B. God made man's soul to be the servant to serve and obey the spirit.

C. God made the body to be a slave, to carry out the wishes of the spirit, directed by the soul.

As long as Adam lived by his spirit and his being was dominated by his spirit he had perfect fellowship with God, with his environment, and with himself. He was a whole person. He was well adjusted. He was supremely happy.

7. SPIRIT, SOUL, AND BODY

Man is made in the image and likeness of God, tripartite: spirit, soul, and body.

A. His soul is tripartite (divisible):

1) His will, the part of his mind that makes decisions, volitional
2) His mind, the part of his intellect that thinks, intellectual
3) His emotions, the part of him that feels, emotional

Try as you will, you will not find a fourth component of the soul any more than you can add to the Godhead, or add a fourth component to spirit, soul, and body.

B.   The spirit can also be divided into three components:

1)   Intuition, knowing without thinking it through, as does the intellect
2)   Communion, fellowship with the Father and with His Son
3)   Conscience, bearing witness with the Spirit; or grieving, quenching, or resisting the Holy Spirit (See Romans 9:1, Ephesians 4:30, I Thessalonians 5:19, and Acts 7:51)

8.   HOW THEY FUNCTION

A.   Body and soul are subject to death because of sin: the body to disintegration, and the soul to separation from God.

B.   The spirit is the substance of God. God is the Father of spirits.

Hebrews 12:9, *Futhermore we have had fathers of our flesh which corrected us, and we gave them reverence: shall we not much rather be in subjection unto the Father of spirits, and live?*

C.   The spirit in the unregenerated human is dead, alienated from God, inactive, and nonrelated, but not extinct.

D.   The spirit, once renewed, is alive. It's clothed with soul and body which are mediums of expression for the spirit.

E.   The natural soul is manifested and sustained in this life by the body. A sick body can destroy the manifestation of the mind, the emotions, and the will.

F.   The human spirit enters reality by the soul and body. The spirit exits the human body by natural death or sin!

The impartation of eternal life is through the engrafted seed of the living Christ.

1)   James 1:21, *Wherefore lay apart all filthiness and superfluity of naughtiness, and receive with meekness the engrafted word, which is able to save your souls.*
2)   I Peter 1:23, *Being born again, not of corruptible seed, but of incorruptible, by the word of God, which liveth and abideth for ever.*

The incorruptible seed is the deathless vehicle for soul and body--the spirit.

9. CONSCIENCE IS SPIRIT

By it we know the laws of God.

A.   It dictates law to the soul, which enforces it.

B.   The modern world is void of pure conscience, but lives by soulish mental powers or methods. The soul looks for numbers to count; the spirit seeks the fruit of holiness, peace, and joy.

10. THERE IS SOMETHING WITHIN MAN THAT CRIES OUT TO GOD

A.   There are three main words that describe the nature of man: spirit, soul, and body. God needs all of us.

B.   Man through his body, can contact the outward world. Through his bodily senses he is world-conscious, or earth-conscious.

C.   Man, through his soul is conscious of himself, and is able to know himself. Through his soul, he is self-conscious or Adam-conscious.

D.   Man, through the human spirit, has the capacity to know God. Through his human spirit, he possesses the capacity to be God-conscious and receives revelation or intuition.

11. MAN'S THREE-FOLD EXPRESSION

Our three-fold personality can be compared to a corporation.

A.   The plant: In the factory there may be a large assembly room where many people are working at producing the finished articles. This department would be comparable to the human body.

B.   The office: There is also the business office where secretaries and various assistants are working. It is a place where correspondence is answered, orders are made, and decisions are carried out. This would compare to the human soul.

C.   The president: Last of all, there is the inner office where the president of the firm resides. In this main office, all the major policies and decisions are made. The main office would illustrate the functions of the human spirit.

In the fallen man, however, the governing office has been taken from the spirit, and transferred to the soul or the body.

When man is unsaved, the heart of man is not identified with the inner spirit, but with man's mind or body. The mind or the body was never meant to rule the personality.

An artist once said, "Well, as far as I am concerned, art is my god." He was knowingly transgressing the first commandment by that kind of attitude. His heart was in painting and drawing pictures. If that man's artistic skill had been taken out of his life, it would, as we sometimes say, have taken the heart out of him.

While on board a ship through the Inside Passage to Alaska, I once asked the captain, "What do you think of Christ? Whose son is He?" The captain said, "Those stars are my gods, sir. Since I was a small boy, I have lived on the high seas, and night after night those wonderful stars have guided my boat. They have never led me astray. To me they are the most beautiful things in the world. I admire them deeply, and perhaps even worship them." I asked him, "But, who made your sparkling gods up there? Who organized and superintends their functions to guarantee that they stay in their orbits and remain faithful to you?" "I do not know," he said, "and am not sure that anyone else knows." "Captain," I said, "my God made your gods."

12. HEART AND SPIRIT

When a person feels the claims of Christ to rule him, and at the same time sets his heart on some sinful affection, his condition produces a divided heart. We discover this truth when we have to make a decision on spiritual issues. What is going to be the ruling center of our lives? A divided heart must choose who is going to rule.

The heart can be involved in an alien interest, affection, possessions, ambitions, or reputation. These can claim the heart and control the personality.

No matter what choice is made, the heart does not lose its moral contact with the conscience, which is part of the human spirit.

Even when the heart is far from God, the spiritual capacity of conscience remains in man and makes itself known in a man's thoughts and feelings.

Here we see the difference between the scriptural words for heart and spirit. These words are often used in the same verse in Scripture. One example is found in Psalm 34:18, *The LORD is nigh unto them that are of a broken heart; and saveth such as be of a contrite spirit.*

There is a scriptural difference between the two words "heart" and "spirit." Perhaps the main difference is that the heart is always the ruling center of the personality. Everything in a man is related to his heart.

CONCLUSION:

Proverbs 4:23, *Keep thy heart with all diligence; for out of it are the issues of life.*

The word "spirit" does not necessarily indicate the ruling disposition, but rather, the spiritual capacity that every man has for God.

The spirit ought to be the ruling center of the personality. However, even when God does not rule in man's spirit, the spiritual capacity still remains.

NOTES

STUDY GUIDE

INDIANA CHRISTIAN UNIVERSITY

CHRISTIAN FOUNDATIONS

Lesson 6 —

THE MINISTRY OF
THE LAYING ON OF HANDS

INTRODUCTION:

A.   The amazing and remarkable human hand consists of 27 bones! It is made up of the *carpus,* which is the wrist, and the *metacarpus,* or the palm of the hand. It also has the four digits or fingers, plus the thumb.

B.   The human hand has 35 muscles and tendons.

C.   Beyond mechanical achievement, the human hand is fearfully and wonderfully made. It can play the piano, build a house, or drive a car.

D.   The human hand is the end of the arm. It is adept at making delicate motions and vibrations and is the center of touch and feeling.

E.   There are four types of nerve endings that make the digit-fingers and the thumb very sensitive.

F.   Blind people rely heavily upon their sense of touch. They can read and find their way with it and the deaf and blind sometimes touch human lips with their fingers and understand what is spoken.

G.   You lift your hands to surrender at war.

H.   You raise your hands to praise God.

I.   Palm analysts claim to be able to read your fortune and future by the lines, creases and wrinkles in the palm of your hand.

J.   The hand is used in so many ways. In a non-religious way, I have seen hands laid on as a greeting, placing a hand on a shoulder or arm. Grown-ups love to place their hands on a child's head.

K. Many pianists and artists have long, elegant hands which make them more adept at their business.

L. A boxer may have large, muscled hands.

M. The long-time farmer probably has gnarled hands.

N. The Bible says a lot about hands.

    1) Matthew 19:13, 15, *Then were there brought unto him little children, that he should put his hands on them, and pray: and the disciples rebuked them.*

        v. 15, *And he laid his hands on them, and departed thence.*

    2) Mark 6:2, *And when the sabbath day was come, he began to teach in the synagogue: and many hearing him were astonished, saying, From whence hath this man these things? and what wisdom is this which is given unto him, that even such mighty works are wrought by his hands?*

    3) Luke 4:40, *Now when the sun was setting, all they that had any sick with divers diseases brought them unto him; and he laid his hands on every one of them, and healed them.*

O. God has hands.

    1) God's hand wrote the law on Mt. Sinai.

        Exodus 31:18, *And he gave unto Moses, when he had made an end of communing with him upon mount Sinai, two tables of testimony, tables of stone, written with the finger of God.*

    2) God's hand overshadowed Moses.

        Exodus 33:22, *And it shall come to pass, while my glory passeth by, that I will put thee in a clift of the rock, and will cover thee with my hand while I pass by.*

    3) God's hand wrote on the wall of Babylon.

        Daniel 5:5, *In the same hour came forth fingers of a man's hand, and wrote over against the candlestick upon the plaster of the wall of the king's palace: and the king saw the part of the hand that wrote.*

        Belshazzar and his empire died that night.

The Ministry of the Laying on of Hands
Lesson 6

READING:

Hebrews 1:10, *And, Thou, Lord, in the beginning hast laid the foundation of the earth; and the heavens are the works of thine hands.*

1.   RITUALS AND ORDINANCES OF THE CHURCH

Christianity has several important rituals.

A.   The Holy Communion, the ordinance of the Lord's Supper

I Corinthians 11:23-26, *For I have received of the Lord that which also I delivered unto you, That the Lord Jesus the same night in which he was betrayed took bread:*
v. 24, *And when he had given thanks, he brake it, and said, Take, eat: this is my body, which is broken for you: this do in remembrance of me.*
v. 25, *After the same manner also he took the cup, when he had supped, saying, This cup is the new testament in my blood: this do ye, as oft as ye drink it, in remembrance of me.*
v. 26, *For as often as ye eat this bread, and drink this cup, ye do shew the Lord's death till he come.*

B.   Water Baptism, the ordinance of immersion

1)   Matthew 28:19, *Go ye therefore, and teach all nations, baptizing them in the name of the Father, and of the Son, and of the Holy Ghost.*

2)   Romans 6:3-5, *Know ye not, that so many of us as were baptized into Jesus Christ were baptized into his death?*
v. 4, *Therefore we are buried with him by baptism into death: that like as Christ was raised up from the dead by the glory of the Father, even so we also should walk in newness of life.*
v. 5, *For if we have been planted together in the likeness of his death, we shall be also in the likeness of his resurrection.*

C.   Laying on of Hands, an act of physical contact

Hebrews 6:2 lists laying on of hands as one of the six foundation truths of the church.

Hebrews 6:2, *Of the doctrine of baptisms, and of laying on of hands, and of resurrection of the dead, and of eternal judgment.*

D. Foot Washing

John 13:13-15, *Ye call me Master and Lord: and ye say well; for so I am.*
v. 14, *If I then, your Lord and Master, have washed your feet; ye also ought to wash one another's feet.*
v. 15, *For I have given you an example, that ye should do as I have done to you.*

2. THE HISTORY OF LAYING ON OF HANDS

A. Man was created by God. Elohim made Adam with His hands (not wings or feet). God gave Adam hands!

B. Human hands

1) A mother's hands are soft and tender, comforting and healing.
2) A baby's hands are beautiful and perfect.
3) The gnarled hands of the craftsman are rugged and callused.
4) A physician's hands of discipline

C. Consider God's power in your hands.

Oral Roberts feels God's power in his hands. William Branham's hands changed color and bumps appeared as a sign of God's power. I saw them.

D. The power of hands

At the funeral of a small boy, the friends came by and gently laid a hand on the father's shoulder.

My mother laid hands on our sick cow when I was a boy and it was healed.

E. The right hand of fellowship

II Kings 10:15, *And when he was departed thence, he lighted on Jehonadab the son of Rechab coming to meet him: and he saluted him, and said to him, Is thine heart right, as my heart is with thy heart? And Jehonadab answered, It is. If it be, give me thine hand. And he gave him his hand; and he took him up to him into the chariot.*

A handshake can reveal personality.

A wholehearted handshake gives the entire hand with vigor. A cold handshake may be with the fingertip, and even that is quickly drawn back.

INDIANA CHRISTIAN UNIVERSITY

CHRISTIAN FOUNDATIONS

Lesson 7

THE MINISTRY OF THE LAYING ON OF HANDS FOR LABOR

INTRODUCTION:

The laying on of hands is not an isolated truth, but is related to total truth. It is an integral part of Christian faith and doctrine. The laying on of hands can influence life and destiny.

READING:

Acts 13:3, *And when they had fasted and prayed, and laid their hands on them, they sent them away.*

1. THE LAYING ON OF HANDS FOR THE MINISTRY OF APOSTLESHIP

    The church fasted and prayed and then laid hands on Saul and Barnabus for missionary labors.

    Acts 13:2-3, *As they ministered to the Lord, and fasted, the Holy Ghost said, Separate me Barnabas and Saul for the work whereunto I have called them.*
    v. 3, *And when they had fasted and prayed, and laid their hands on them, they sent them away.*

2. THE LAYING ON OF HANDS FOR THE LAYMAN'S LABOR

    The deacons were set aside. The apostles prayed and then laid hands on the deacons.

Acts 6:1-6, *And in those days, when the number of the disciples was multiplied, there arose a murmuring of the Grecians against the Hebrews, because their widows were neglected in the daily ministration.*

v. 2, *Then the twelve called the multitude of the disciples unto them, and said, It is not reason that we should leave the word of God, and serve tables.*

v. 3, *Wherefore, brethren, look ye out among you seven men of honest report, full of the Holy Ghost and wisdom, whom we may appoint over this business.*

v. 4, *But we will give ourselves continually to prayer, and to the ministry of the word.*

v. 5, *And the saying pleased the whole multitude: and they chose Stephen, a man full of faith and of the Holy Ghost, and Philip, and Prochorus, and Nicanor, and Timon, and Parmenas, and Nicolas a proselyte of Antioch:*

v. 6, *Whom they set before the apostles: and when they had prayed, they laid their hands on them.*

3. LAYING ON HANDS FOR THE MINISTRY GIFTS

The presbytery laid hands on Timothy for ministry.

A.   Timothy 4:14, *Neglect not the gift that is in thee, which was given thee by prophecy, with the laying on of the hands of the presbytery.*

B.   Timothy 5:22, *Lay hands suddenly on no man, neither be partaker of other men's sins: keep thyself pure.*

C.   Timothy 1:6, *Wherefore I put thee in remembrance that thou stir up the gift of God, which is in thee by the putting on of my hands.*

4. LAYING ON OF HANDS FOR POSITION

A.   To set aside leaders, authority.

Numbers 27:18, *And the LORD said unto Moses, Take thee Joshua the son of Nun, a man in whom is the spirit, and lay thine hand upon him.*

B.   God commanded Moses to lay his hand upon Joshua. It symbolized the transfer of authority.

Deuteronomy 34:9, *And Joshua the son of Nun was full of the spirit of wisdom; for Moses had laid his hands upon him: and the children of Israel hearkened unto him, and did as the LORD commanded Moses.*

5. **LAYING ON HANDS TO RECEIVE THE BAPTISM OF THE HOLY SPIRIT**

    Three of these were by the laying on of hands.

    A. Acts 8:14-15, 17, *Now when the apostles which were at Jerusalem heard that Samaria had received the word of God, they sent unto them Peter and John:*

        v. 15, *Who, when they were come down, prayed for them, that they might receive the Holy Ghost:*

        v. 17, *Then laid they their hands on them, and they received the Holy Ghost.*

    B. Acts 9:17, *And Ananias went his way, and entered into the house; and putting his hands on him said, Brother Saul, the Lord, even Jesus, that appeared unto thee in the way as thou camest, hath sent me, that thou mightest receive thy sight, and be filled with the Holy Ghost.*

    C. Acts 19:1, 6, . . .*it came to pass, that, while Apollos was at Corinth, Paul having passed through the upper coasts came to Ephesus: and finding certain disciples,*

        v. 6, *And when Paul had laid his hands upon them, the Holy Ghost came on them; and they spake with tongues, and prophesied.*

6. **GOD USED PAUL'S HANDS TO DO SPECIAL MIRACLES.**

    Acts 19:11, *And God wrought special miracles by the hands of Paul.*

7. **JACOB LAID HIS HAND UPON JOSEPH'S SONS FOR PARENTAL BLESSING.**

    Genesis 48:14, *And Israel stretched out his right hand, and laid it upon Ephraim's head, who was the younger, and his left hand upon Manasseh's head, guiding his hands wittingly; for Manasseh was the firstborn.*

8. **WHEN YOU STUDY THE WORLD**

    The devil counterfeits God's program.

    A. Witches lay on hands.

    B. The witch doctors use their hands to carry on witchcraft.

    C. God's part is true, honest, and powerful.

NOTES

_____

_____

_____

_____

_____

_____

_____

_____

_____

_____

_____

_____

_____

_____

_____

_____

_____

_____

_____

_____

_____

_____

_____

STUDY GUIDE

INDIANA CHRISTIAN UNIVERSITY

CHRISTIAN FOUNDATIONS

Lesson 8

JESUS AND THE LAYING ON OF HANDS

INTRODUCTION:

In this great and final commission to the church before re-entering Heaven and taking His place on the throne of the Most High, Jesus stated several absolutes. He included the ministering and the power of the laying on of hands for the healing of the sick.

READING:

Mark 16:14-18, *Afterward he appeared unto the eleven as they sat at meat and upbraided them with their unbelief and hardness of heart because they believed not them which had seen him after he was risen.*
v. 15, *And he said unto them, Go ye into all the world and preach the gospel to every creature.*
v. 16, *He that believeth and is baptized shall be saved but he that believeth not shall be damned.*
v. 17, *And these signs shall follow them that believe; In my name shall they cast out devils; they shall speak with new tongues;*
v. 18, *They shall take up serpents; and if they drink any deadly thing it shall not hurt them; they shall lay hands on the sick and they shall recover.*

1. THE LORD JESUS LAID HANDS ON HUMANITY TO BLESS

    A. Jairus' daughter was dead.

        Matthew 9:18-25, *While he spake these things unto them, behold, there came a certain ruler, and worshipped him, saying, My daughter is even now dead: but come and lay thy hand upon her, and she shall live.*

45

v. 19, *And Jesus arose, and followed him, and so did his disciples.*
v. 20, *And, behold, a woman, which was diseased with an issue of blood twelve years, came behind him, and touched the hem of his garment:*
v. 21, *For she said within herself, If I may but touch his garment, I shall be whole.*
v. 22, *But Jesus turned him about, and when he saw her, he said, Daughter, be of good comfort; thy faith hath made thee whole. And the woman was made whole from that hour.*
v. 23, *And when Jesus came into the ruler's house, and saw the minsterls and the people making a noise,*
v. 24, *He said unto them, Give place: for the maid is not dead, but sleepeth. And they laughed him to scorn.*
v. 25, *But when the people were put forth, he went in, and took her by the hand, and the maid arose.*

B. Jesus laid hands on Peter's mother-in-law.

Matthew 8:15, *And he touched her hand and the fever left her: and she arose and ministered unto them.*

C. Jesus laid hands upon lepers.

Mark 1:40-42, *And there came a leper to him, beseeching him, and kneeling down to him, and saying unto him, If thou wilt, thou canst make me clean.*
v. 41, *And Jesus, moved with compassion, put forth his hand, and touched him, and saith unto him, I will; be thou clean.*
v. 42, *And, as soon as he had spoken, immediately the leprosy departed from him, and he was cleansed.*

D. Jesus laid hands upon a group of children.

1) Matthew 19:1-2, 13-14, *And it came to pass, that when Jesus had finished these sayings, he departed from Galilee, and came into the coast of Judæa beyond Jordan;*
v. 2, *And great multitudes followed him; and he healed them there.*

v. 13, *Then were there brought unto him little children, that he should put his hands on them, and pray: and the disciples rebuked them.*
v. 14, *But Jesus said, Suffer little children, and forbid them not, to come unto me: for of such is the kingdom of heaven.*

2) Mark 10:16, *And he took them up in his arms, put his hands upon them, and blessed them.*

E. Jesus healed those sick with divers diseases.

Luke 4:40, *Now when the sun was setting, all they that had any sick with divers diseases brought them unto him; and he laid his hands on every one of them, and healed them.*

F. Jesus laid hands on a woman who had a spirit of infirmity.

Luke 13:13, *And he laid his hands on her: and immediately she was made straight, and glorified God.*

G. Jesus laid His hands on a few sick people and healed them.

Mark 6:5, *And he could there do no mighty work, save that he laid his hands upon a few sick folk, and healed them.*

H. Deaf man with impediment in speech

Mark 7:32, 35, *And they bring unto him one that was deaf, and had an impediment in his speech; and they beseech him to put his hand upon him.*

v. 35, *And straightway his ears were opened, and the string of his tongue was loosed, and he spake plain.*

I. Jesus laid hands on a blind man.

Mark 8:22-25, *And he cometh to Bethsaida: and they bring a blind man unto him, and besought him to touch him.*
v. 23, *And he took the blind man by the hand, and led him out of the town; and when he had spit on his eyes, and put his hands upon him, he asked him if he saw ought.*
v. 24, *And he looked up, and said, I see men as trees, walking.*
v. 25, *After that he put his hands again upon his eyes, and made him look up: and he was restored, and saw every man clearly.*

So the blind man was brought to Jesus. After the first touch, he saw men as trees walking. When Jesus laid hands on him a second time, his vision was restored.

NOTES

STUDY GUIDE

INDIANA CHRISTIAN UNIVERSITY

CHRISTIAN FOUNDATIONS

Lesson 9

WHO SHOULD LAY HANDS ON WHOM?

INTRODUCTION:

The Scripture admonishes believers to practice laying on of hands, but we should be cautious about whom we allow to lay hands on us.

READING:

Mark 16:17-18, *And these signs shall follow them that believe; In my name shall they cast out devils; they shall speak with new tongues;*
v. 18, *They shall take up serpents; and if they drink any deadly thing, it shall not hurt them; they shall lay hands on the sick, and they shall recover.*

1. ### THE INDONESIAN CHRISTIANS LAY HANDS ON THE DEAD

   They are raised. There are many occurrences on record of the Indonesian Christians praying for and seeing the dead raised. One Indonesian pastor who was visiting me said he had personally raised twelve people from the dead.

2. ### THE DEVIL DOES IT AS A RITUAL

   The devil does it as a ritual, but his hands are bad hands; they are satanic. In witchcraft, hands are laid on for demonic worship. Be careful who lays hands on you. Do not let spiritists, mediums of any kind, or people with wrong doctrines, lay hands on you. A woman in Brazil had hands laid on her belly before the birth of her baby so that he would have the power to serve Satan as a witch doctor.

3.   HANDS HAVE BEEN LAID ON ME

In my own life, I have had hands laid on me for the imparting of spiritual gifts and the establishment into position of ministry.

A.   At my ordination

Rev. Ernest Williams laid hands on me in an ordination service at Little Rock, Arkansas. It was a significant event and the blessing of it has remained with me through more than 50 years of ministry.

B.   For missionary anointing

At the time I met Howard Carter in Eureka Springs, Arkansas, he and Stanley Frodsham, the editor of the *Pentecostal Evangel,* laid hands on me for a blessing on my life as a missionary. It was a thrilling anointing for my spirit, soul, and body.

C.   By Smith Wigglesworth

In Great Britain, I was with Smith Wigglesworth in many conferences, special meetings, and in his home. The last time he laid hands on me was different from all the other times. He prayed, "Lord, grant that my spirit will rest on Lester Sumrall."

STUDY GUIDE

INDIANA CHRISTIAN UNIVERSITY

CHRISTIAN FOUNDATIONS

Lesson 10

WHY WE BELIEVE IN SALVATION

INTRODUCTION:

God placed Adam in the Garden of Eden and had communion with him there daily. When Adam sinned, this communion ceased. Adam not only lost his place in the Garden, but Romans 5:12 declares, *Wherefore, as by one man sin entered into the world, and death by sin; and so death passed upon all men, for that all have sinned.* Through salvation God has restored man to a place of fellowship and communion and given back to him blessings and benefits that were lost when Adam transgressed against God.

READING:

John 3:1-3, *There was a man of the Pharisees, named Nicodemus, a ruler of the Jews:*
v. 2, *The same came to Jesus by night, and said unto him, Rabbi, we know that thou art a teacher come from God: for no man can do these miracles that thou doest, except God be with him.*
v. 3, *Jesus answered and said unto him, Verily, verily, I say unto thee, Except a man be born again, he cannot see the kingdom of God.*

1. GOD'S PART IN SALVATION

    A. He loves us.

        1) Romans 5:8, *But God commendeth his love toward us, in that, while we were yet sinners, Christ died for us.*

        2) John 3:16, *For God so loved the world, that he gave his only begotten Son, that whosoever believeth in him should not perish, but have everlasting life.*

        3) Jeremiah 31:3, *The Lord hath appeared of old unto me, saying, Yea, I have loved thee with an everlasting love: therefore with lovingkindness have I drawn thee.*

B.   God is concerned about us.

    1)   Isaiah 1:18, *Come now, and let us reason together, saith the LORD: though your sins be as scarlet, they shall be as white as snow; though they be red like crimson, they shall be as wool.*

    2)   II Peter 3:9, *The Lord is not slack concerning his promise, as some men count slackness; but is longsuffering to us-ward, not willing that any should perish, but that all should come to repentance.*

    3)   Romans 15:4, *For whatsoever things were written aforetime were written for our learning, that we through patience and comfort of the scriptures might have hope.*

C.   God has given all an opportunity.

Romans 10:11-13, *For the scripture saith, Whosoever believeth on him shall not be ashamed.*
v. 12, *For there is no difference between the Jew and the Greek: for the same Lord over all is rich unto all that call upon him.*
v. 13, *For whosoever shall call upon the name of the Lord shall be saved.*

D.   He will perform that which He has promised.

    1)   Romans 4:21, *And being fully persuaded that, what he had promised, he was able also to perform.*

    2)   Titus 1:2, *In hope of eternal life, which God, that cannot lie, promised before the world began.*

2.   CHRIST'S PART IN SALVATION

A.   Christ is able to save.

    1)   Hebrews 7:25, *Wherefore he is able also to save them to the uttermost that come unto God by him, seeing he ever liveth to make intercession for them.*

    2)   Jude 24-25, *Now unto him that is able to keep you from falling, and to present you faultless before the presence of his glory with exceeding joy.*
v. 25, *To the only wise God our Saviour, be glory and majesty, dominion and power, both now and ever. Amen.*

    B.   He is willing to save us.

        1)   I Timothy 1:15, *This is a faithful saying, and worthy of all acceptation, that Christ Jesus came into the world to save sinners; of whom I am chief.*

        2)   Luke 19:10, *For the Son of man is come to seek and to save that which was lost.*

        3)   II Peter 3:9, *The Lord is not slack concerning his promise, as some men count slackness; but is longsuffering to us-ward, not willing that any should perish, but that all should come to repentance.*

    C.   He is ready to save us.

        1)   John 10:9, *I am the door: by me if any man enter in, he shall be saved, and shall go in and out, and find pasture.*

        2)   John 14:6, *Jesus saith unto him, I am the way, the truth, and the life: no man cometh unto the Father, but by me.*

    D.   He has already provided for our salvation.

        1)   Colossians 1:14, *In whom we have redemption through his blood, even the forgiveness of sins.*

        2)   Galatians 3:13, *Christ hath redeemed us from the curse of the law, being made a curse for us: for it is written, Cursed is every one that hangeth on a tree.*

3.   THE HOLY SPIRIT'S PART IN SALVATION

    A.   He calls us to salvation.

        1)   Revelation 22:17, *And the Spirit and the bride say, Come. And let him that heareth say, Come. And let him that is athirst come. And whosoever will, let him take the water of life freely.*

        2)   Hebrews 3:7-8, *Wherefore (as the Holy Ghost saith, Today if ye will hear his voice,*
            v. 8, *Harden not your hearts, as in the provocation, in the day of temptation in the wilderness:*

B.   He works for us and in us.

1)   Romans 5:5, *And hope maketh not ashamed; because the love of God is shed abroad in our hearts by the Holy Ghost which is given unto us.*

2)   John 16:8-9, *And when he is come, he will reprove the world of sin, and of righteousness, and of judgment:*
v. 9, *Of sin, because they believe not on me. . .*

3)   Titus 3:5, *Not by works of righteousness which we have done, but according to his mercy he saved us, by the washing of regeneration, and renewing of the Holy Ghost.*

C.   Without Him we can do nothing.

1)   Zechariah 4:6, *. . .Not by might, nor by power, but by my spirit, saith the LORD of hosts.*

2)   I Corinthians 12:3, *Wherefore I give you to understand, that no man speaking by the Spirit of God calleth Jesus accursed: and that no man can say that Jesus is the Lord, but by the Holy Ghost.*

D.   He gives assurance.

1)   I Thessalonians 1:5, *For our gospel came not unto you in word only, but also in power, and in the Holy Ghost, and in much assurance; as ye know what manner of men we were among you for your sake.*

2)   I John 3:24, *And he that keepeth his commandments dwelleth in him, and he in him. And hereby we know that he abideth in us, by the Spirit which he hath given us.*

3)   Romans 8:16, *The Spirit itself beareth witness with our spirit, that we are the children of God:*

4.   OUR PART IN SALVATION

A.   We must repent of our sins.

1)   Luke 13:5, *I tell you, Nay: but, except ye repent, ye shall all likewise perish.*

2)   II Corinthians 7:10, *For godly sorrow worketh repentance to salvation not to be repented of: but the sorrow of the world worketh death.*

B. We must humble ourselves.

1) Matthew 18:3, *And said, Verily I say unto you, Except ye be converted, and become as little children, ye shall not enter into the kingdom of heaven.*

2) I Peter 5:5-6, *Likewise, ye younger, submit yourselves unto the elder. Yea, all of you be subject one to another, and be clothed with humility: for God resisteth the proud, and giveth grace to the humble.*
v. 6, *Humble yourselves therefore under the mighty hand of God, that he may exalt you in due time.*

C. We must have faith in Christ.

1) Ephesians 2:8, *For by grace are ye saved through faith; and that not of yourselves: it is the gift of God.*

2) Hebrews 11:6, *But without faith it is impossible to please him: for he that cometh to God must believe that he is, and that he is a rewarder of them that diligently seek him.*

3) James 1:6, *But let him ask in faith, nothing wavering. For he that wavereth is like a wave of the sea driven with the wind and tossed.*

D. Confess Jesus Christ as Lord and Savior.

Romans 10:9-10, *That if thou shalt confess with thy mouth the Lord Jesus, and shalt believe in thine heart that God hath raised him from the dead, thou shalt be saved.*
v. 10, *For with the heart man believeth unto righteousness; and with the mouth confession is made unto salvation.*

E. We must obey God's Word.

1) Hebrews 5:9, *And being made perfect, he became the author of eternal salvation unto all of them that obey him.*

2) II Thessalonians 1:7-8, *And to you who are troubled rest with us, when the Lord Jesus shall be revealed from heaven with his mighty angels.*
v. 8, *In flaming fire taking vengeance on them that know not God, and that obey not the gospel of our Lord Jesus Christ.*

5.   HOW SHALL WE ESCAPE . . .

After we have heard the Gospel, that Christ died for our sins, that He was buried, and that He rose again, *How shall we escape, if we neglect so great salvation* (Hebrews 2:3).

STUDY GUIDE

INDIANA CHRISTIAN UNIVERSITY

CHRISTIAN FOUNDATIONS

Lesson 11

WHY WE BELIEVE IN
THE BAPTISM OF THE HOLY SPIRIT

INTRODUCTION:

The fact of a Spirit baptism in Scripture is very clear. In Matthew 3:11, John the Baptist said to his followers concerning Christ, . . .*he shall baptize you with the Holy Ghost, and with fire.* In Acts 1:5, Jesus said to His disciples just before Pentecost, . . .*ye shall be baptized with the Holy Ghost not many days hence.*

READING:

Acts 2:1-4, *And when the day of Pentecost was fully come, they were all with one accord in one place.*
v. 2, *And suddenly there came a sound from heaven as of a rushing mighty wind, and it filled all the house where they were sitting.*
v. 3, *And there appeared unto them cloven tongues like as of fire, and it sat upon each of them.*
v. 4, *And they were all filled with the Holy Ghost, and began to speak with other tongues, as the Spirit gave them utterance.*

1.   BAPTISM OF THE HOLY SPIRIT IN PROPHECY

   A.   Isaiah spoke of this as a rest and a refreshing.

      Isaiah 28:11-12, . . .*with stammering lips and another tongue will he speak to this people.*
      v. 12, *To whom he said, This is the rest wherewith ye may cause the weary to rest; and this is the refreshing: yet they would not hear.*

B. Joel prophesied the outpouring of the Spirit.

Joel 2:28-29, *And it shall come to pass afterward, that I will pour out my spirit upon all flesh; and your sons and your daughters shall prophesy, your old men shall dream dreams, your young men shall see visions:*
v. 29, *And also upon the servants and upon the handmaids in those days will I pour out my spirit.*

C. John the Baptist foretold the baptism with the Spirit.

Matthew 3:11, *I indeed baptize you with water unto repentance: but he that cometh after me is mightier than I, whose shoes I am not worthy to bear: he shall baptize you with the Holy Ghost, and with fire.*

D. Peter connected Joel's prophecy with the happenings in the Upper Room on the Day of Pentecost.

Acts 2:16-18, *But this is that which was spoken by the prophet Joel;*
v. 17, *And it shall come to pass in the last days, saith God, I will pour out of my Spirit upon all flesh: and your sons and your daughters shall prophesy, and your young men shall see visions, and your old men shall dream dreams:*
v. 18, *And on my servants and on my handmaidens I will pour out in those days of my Spirit; and they shall prophesy.*

2. WHAT IS THE BAPTISM OF THE HOLY SPIRIT?

A. It is being baptized with or in the Holy Spirit. The Greek word *baptidzo* means "to bury."

1) Mark 1:8, *I indeed have baptized you with water: but he shall baptize you with the Holy Ghost.*

2) Luke 3:16, *John answered, saying unto them all, I indeed baptize you with water; but one mightier than I cometh, the latchet of whose shoes I am not worthy to unloose: he shall baptize you with the Holy Ghost and with fire.*

B. It is accepting the promised Comforter.

John 14:16-17, *And I will pray the Father, and he shall give you another Comforter, that he may abide with you for ever;*
v. 17, *Even the Spirit of truth; whom the world cannot receive, because it seeth him not, neither knoweth him: but ye know him; for he dwelleth with you, and shall be in you.*

C.   It is being filled and indwelt by the third person of the Trinity.

Acts 2:4, *And they were all filled with the Holy Ghost, and began to speak with other tongues, as the Spirit gave them utterance.*

D.   At conversion, we receive the Spirit of God's Son.

1)   Galatians 4:6, *And because ye are sons, God hath sent forth the Spirit of his Son into your hearts, crying, Abba, Father.*

2)   Romans 8:15, *For ye have not received the spirit of bondage again to fear; but ye have received the Spirit of adoption, whereby we cry, Abba, Father.*

3)   Romans 8:9, *But ye are not in the flesh, but in the Spirit, if so be that the Spirit of God dwell in you. Now if any man have not the Spirit of Christ, he is none of his.*

4)   Mark 14:36, *And he said, Abba, Father, all things are possible unto thee; take away this cup from me: nevertheless not what I will, but what thou wilt.*

E.   At conversion, we are born of the Spirit.

1)   John 1:11-13, *He came unto his own, and his own received him not.*
v. 12, *But as many as received him, to them gave he power to become the sons of God, even to them that believe on his name:*
v. 13, *Which were born, not of blood, nor of the will of the flesh, nor of the will of man, but of God.*

2)   John 3:5-6, *Jesus answered, Verily, verily, I say unto thee, Except a man be born of water and of the Spirit, he cannot enter into the kingdom of God.*
v. 6, *That which is born of the flesh is flesh; and that which is born of the Spirit is spirit.*

F.   At the Holy Spirit baptism, we receive the Holy Spirit sent by the Son from the Father.

1)   John 15:26, *But when the Comforter is come, whom I will send unto you from the Father, even the Spirit of truth, which proceedeth from the Father, he shall testify of me.*

2)   Acts 2:32-33, *This Jesus hath God raised up, whereof we all are witnesses.*
     v. 33, *Therefore being by the right hand of God exalted, and having received of the Father the promise of the Holy Ghost, he hath shed forth this, which ye now see and hear.*

3.   THE INITIAL EVIDENCE OF RECEIVING THE HOLY SPIRIT

A.   Speaking in tongues was the evidence at Pentecost.

Acts 2:4, *And they were all filled with the Holy Ghost, and began to speak with other tongues, as the Spirit gave them utterance.*

B.   Speaking in tongues was the evidence at the house of Cornelius.

Acts 10:44-48, *While Peter yet spake these words, the Holy Ghost fell on all them which heard the word.*
v. 45, *And they of the circumcision which believed were astonished, as many as came with Peter, because that on the Gentiles also was poured out the gift of the Holy Ghost.*
v. 46, *For they heard them speak with tongues, and magnify God. Then answered Peter,*
v. 47, *Can any man forbid water, that these should not be baptized, which have received the Holy Ghost as well as we?*
v. 48, *And he commanded them to be baptized in the name of the Lord. Then prayed they him to tarry certain days.*

C.   Speaking in tongues was the evidence at Ephesus.

Acts 19:6, *And when Paul had laid his hands upon them, the Holy Ghost came on them; and they spake with tongues, and prophesied.*

D.   Paul was filled with the Holy Spirit.

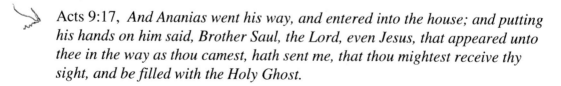

Acts 9:17, *And Ananias went his way, and entered into the house; and putting his hands on him said, Brother Saul, the Lord, even Jesus, that appeared unto thee in the way as thou camest, hath sent me, that thou mightest receive thy sight, and be filled with the Holy Ghost.*

E.   Paul spoke with tongues more than all.

I Corinthians 14:18, *I thank my God, I speak with tongues more than ye all.*

4.   THE RESULTS OF RECEIVING THE HOLY SPIRIT

A.   Power to witness

Acts 1:8, *But ye shall receive power, after that the Holy Ghost is come upon you: and ye shall be witnesses unto me both in Jerusalem, and in all Judæa, and in Samaria, and unto the utter most part of the earth.*

1)   Acts 4:13, *Now when they saw the boldness of Peter and John, and perceived that they were unlearned and ignorant men, they marvelled; and they took knowledge of them, that they had been with Jesus.*

2)   Acts 6:10, *And they were not able to resist the wisdom and the spirit by which he spake.*

B.   Miraculous power with signs and wonders

Mark 16:17-18, *And these signs shall follow them that believe; In my name shall they cast out devils; they shall speak with new tongues;*
v. 18, *They shall take up serpents; and if they drink any deadly thing, it shall not hurt them; they shall lay hands on the sick, and they shall recover.*

C.   Deepened prayer life

1)   Romans 8:26, *Likewise the Spirit also helpeth our infirmities: for we know not what we should pray for as we ought: but the Spirit itself maketh intercession for us with groanings which cannot be uttered.*

2)   Ephesians 6:18, *Praying always with all prayer and supplication in the Spirit, and watching thereunto with all perseverance and supplication for all saints;*

3)   Jude 20, *But ye, beloved, building up yourselves on your most holy faith, praying in the Holy Ghost.*

D.   Ability to overcome the flesh

1)   Galatians 5:16, *This I say then, Walk in the Spirit, and ye shall not fulfil the lust of the flesh.*

2)   Romans 6:12, *Let not sin therefore reign in your mortal body, that ye should obey it in the lusts thereof.*

3) Romans 8:13, *For if ye live after the flesh, ye shall die: but if ye through the Spirit do mortify the deeds of the body, ye shall live.*

4) Romans 13:14, *But put ye on the Lord Jesus Christ, and make not proîvision for the flesh, to fulfil the lusts thereof.*

E. A Comforter who abides forever

John 14:16, *And I will pray the Father, and he shall give you another Comforter, that he may abide with you for ever.*

F. We have a Comforter who is in us.

John 14:17, *Even the Spirit of truth; whom the world cannot receive, because it seeth him not, neither knoweth him: but ye know him; for he dwelleth with you, and shall be in you.*

G. We have a Comforter who testifies of Christ.

John 15:26, *. . .when the Comforter is come, whom I will send unto you from the Father, even the Spirit of truth, which proceedeth from the Father, he shall testify of me.*

H. We have a Comforter who guides us into all truth, shows us things, and glorifies Christ.

John 16:13-14, *Howbeit when he, the Spirit of truth, is come, he will guide you into all truth: for he shall not speak of himself; but whatsoever he shall hear, that shall he speak: and he will shew you things to come.*
v. 14, *He shall glorify me: for he shall receive of mine, and shall shew it unto you.*

STUDY GUIDE

INDIANA CHRISTIAN UNIVERSITY

CHRISTIAN FOUNDATIONS

Lesson 12

WHY WE BELIEVE IN HEALING

INTRODUCTION:

One of the greatest controversies involving healing is whether or not it is part of divine salvation or the atonement of Calvary.

Romans 5:12 declares that, *. . .by one man sin entered into the world, and death by sin. . .* Sickness and death entered the world with sin, as a result of sin. Therefore, healing cannot be a side issue because disease is of the devil as sin is of the devil. Now, since disease entered by sin, its true remedy must be found in the redemption of Christ.

READING:

Matthew 8:1-3, *When he was come down from the mountain, great multitudes followed him.*
v. 2, *And, behold, there came a leper and worshipped him, saying, Lord, if thou wilt, thou canst make me clean.*
v. 3, *And Jesus put forth his hand, and touched him, saying, I will; be thou clean. And immediately his leprosy was cleansed.*

1.   HEALING UNDER PROMISE

   If the children of Israel would keep God's commandments, He would keep disease and sickness from them.

   A.   Exodus 15:26, *And said, If thou wilt diligently hearken to the voice of the LORD thy God, and wilt do that which is right in his sight, and wilt give ear to his commandments, and keep all his statues, I will put none of these diseases upon thee, which I have brought upon the Egyptians: for I am the LORD that healeth thee.*

   B.   Exodus 23:25, *And ye shall serve the LORD your God, and he shall bless thy bread, and thy water; and I will take sickness away from the midst of thee.*

63

2.   HEALING UNDER LAW

A.   The priest made atonement for the cleansing of the leper.

Leviticus 14:18, *And the remnant of the oil that is the priest's hand he shall pour upon the head of him that is to be cleansed: and the priest shall make an atonement for him before the LORD.*

B.   Israelites were healed by looking upon the brazen serpent.

Numbers 21:5-9, *And the people spake against God, and against Moses, Wherefore have ye brought us up out of Egypt to die in the wilderness? for there is no bread, neither is there any water; and our soul loatheth this light bread.*
v. 6, *And the LORD sent fiery serpents among the people, and they bit the people; and much people of Israel died.*
v. 7, *Therefore the people came to Moses, and said, We have sinned, for we have spoken against the LORD, and against thee: pray unto the LORD, that he take away the serpents from us. And Moses prayed for the people.*
v. 8, *And the LORD said unto Moses, Make thee a fiery serpent, and set it upon a pole: and it shall come to pass, that every one that is bitten, when he looketh upon it, shall live.*
v. 9, *And Moses made a serpent of brass, and put it upon a pole, and it came to pass, that if a serpent had bitten any man, when he beheld the serpent of brass, he lived.*

C.   Christ is the anti-type of the brazen serpent.

John 3:14-15, *And as Moses lifted up the serpent in the wilderness, even so must the Son of man be lifted up:*
v. 15, *That whosoever believeth in him should not perish, but have eternal life.*

D.   Naaman healed of leprosy.

II Kings 5:14, *Then went he down, and dipped himself seven times in Jordan, according to the saying of the man of God: and his flesh came again like unto the flesh of a little child, and he was clean.*

3. HEALING UNDER PROPHECY

A. With His stripes we are healed.

Isaiah 53:4-5, *Surely he hath borne our griefs, and carried our sorrows: yet we did esteem him stricken, smitten of God, and afflicted.*
v. 5, *But he was wounded for our transgressions, he was bruised for our iniquities: the chastisement of our peace was upon him; and with his stripes we are healed.*

B. The Sun of righteousness shall rise with healing in His wings.

Malachi 4:2, *But unto you that fear my naem shall the Sun of righteousness arise with healing in his wings; and ye shall go forth, and grow up as calves of the stall.*

C. Christ Himself took our infirmities, and bore our sicknesses.

1) Matthew 8:17, *That it might be fulfilled which was spoken by Esaias the prophet, saying, Himself took our infirmities, and bare our sicknesses.*

2) I Peter 2:24, *Who his own self bare our sins in his own body on the tree, that we, being dead to sins, should live unto righteous-ness: by whose stripes ye were healed.*

4. HEALING UNDER CHRIST

A. He healed all who were oppressed of the devil.

1) Acts 10:38, *How God anointed Jesus of Nazareth with the Holy Ghost and with power: who went about doing good, and healing all that were oppressed of the devil; for God was with him.*

2) Matthew 4:23-24, *And Jesus went about all Galilee, teaching in their synagogues, and preaching the gospel of the kingdom, and helaing all manner of sickness and all manner of disease among the people.*
v. 24, And his fame went throughout all Syria: and they brought unto him all sick people that were taken with divers diseases and torments, and those which were possessed with devils, and those which were lunatick, and those that had the palsy; and he healed them.

3)   Matthew 9:35, *And Jesus went about all the cities and villages, teaching in their synagogues, and preaching the gospel of the kingdom, and healing every sickness and every disease among the people.*

B.   Healing is the children's bread.

Mark 7:27, *But Jesus said unto her, Let the children first be filled: for it is not meet to take the children's bread, and to cast it unto the dogs.*

C.   He cast out devils.

1)   Matthew 9:32-33, *As they went out, behold, they brought to him a dumb man possessed with a devil.*
v. 33, *And when the devil was cast out, the dumb spake: and the multitudes marvelled, saying, It was never so seen in Israel.*

2)   Mark 1:23-26, *And there was in their synagogue a man with an unclean spirit; and he cried out,*
v. 24, *Saying, Let us alone; what have we to do with thee, thou Jesus of Nazareth? art thou come to destroy us? I know thee who thou art, the Holy One of God.*
v. 25, *And Jesus rebuked him, saying, Hold thy peace, and come out of him.*
v. 26, *And when the unclean spirit had torn him, and cried with a loud voice, he came out of him.*

3)   Mark 1:32-34, *And at even, when the sun did set, they brought unto him all that were diseased, and them that were possessed with devils.*
v. 33, *And all the city was gathered together at the door.*
v. 34, *And he healed many that were sick of divers diseases, and cast out many devils; and suffered not the devils to speak, because they knew him.*

D.   He opened blind eyes and unstopped deaf ears.

1)   Matthew 9:28-30, *And when he was come into the house, the blind men came to him: and Jesus saith unto them, Believe ye that I am able to do this? They said unto him, Yea, Lord.*
v. 29, *Then touched he their eyes, saying, According to your faith be it unto you.*
v. 30, *And their eyes were opened; and Jesus straitly charged them, saying, See that no man know it.*

2)   Matthew 12:22, *Then was brought unto him one possessed with a devil, blind, and dumb: and he healed him, insomuch that the blind and dumb both spake and saw.*

E.   He raised the dead.

    1)   Matthew 9:24-25, *He said unto them, Give place: for the maid is not dead, but sleepeth. And they laughed him to scorn.*
v. 25, But when the people were put forth, he went in and took her by the hand, and the maid arose.

    2)   Luke 7:14-15, *And he came and touched the bier: and they that bare him stood still. And he said, Young man, I say unto thee, Arise.*
v. 15, And he that was dead sat up, and began to speak. And he delivered him to his mother.

    3)   John 11:43-44, *And when he thus had spoken, he cried with a loud voice, Lazarus, come forth.*
v. 44, And he that was dead came forth, bound hand and foot with graveclothes: and his face was bound about with a napkin. Jesus saith unto them, Loose him, and let him go.

5.   HEALING UNDER THE APOSTLES

A.   Some were healed by Peter's shadow passing over them.

Acts 5:15, *Insomuch that they brought forth the sick into the streets, and laid them on beds and couches, that at the least the shadow of Peter passing by might overshadow some of them.*

B.   Healing came by handkerchiefs from Paul's body.

Acts 19:12, *So that from his body were brought unto the sick handkerchiefs or aprons, and the diseases departed from them, and the evil spirits went out of them.*

C.   The apostles cast out devils in Jesus' name.

Acts 16:16-18, *And it came to pass, as we went to prayer, a certain damsel possessed with a spirit of divination met us, which brought her masters much gain by soothsaying:*
v. 17, The same followed paul and us, and cried, saying, These men are the servants of the most high God, which shew unto us the way of salvation.
v. 18, And this did she many days. But Paul, being grieved, turned and said to the spirit, I command thee in the name of Jesus Christ to come out of her. And he came out the same hour.

D.   They raised the dead.

1)   Acts 9:40-41, *But Peter put them all forth, and kneeled down, and prayed; and turning him to the body said, Tabitha, arise. And she opened her eyes: and when she saw Peter, she sat up.*
v. 41, And he gave her his hand, and lifted her up, and when he had îcalled the saints and widows, presented her alive.

2)   Acts 20:9-10, 12, *And there sat in a window a certain young man named Eutychus, being fallen into a deep sleep: and as Paul was long preaching, he sunk down with sleep, and fell down from the third loft, and was taken up dead.*
v. 10, And Paul went down, and fell on him, and embracing him said, Trouble not yourselves; for his life is in him.
v. 12, And they brought the young man alive, and were not a little comforted.

6.   HEALING TODAY

A.   Believers shall cast out devils and heal the sick.

Mark 16:17-18, *And these signs shall follow them that believe; In my name shall they cast out devils; they shall speak with new tongues;*
v. 18, They shall take up serpents; and if they drink any deadly thing, it shall not hurt them; they shall lay hands on the sick, and they shall recover.

B.   Anointing with oil and the prayer of faith shall save the sick.

James 5:14-15, *Is any sick among you? let him call for the elders of the church; and let them pray over him, anointing him with oil in the name of the Lord:*
v. 15, And the prayer of faith shall save the sick, and the Lord shall raise him up; and if he have committed sins, they shall be forgiven him.

C.   Confess your faults one to another and pray for one another that ye may be healed.

James 5:16, *Confess your faults one to another, and pray one for another, that ye may be healed. The effectual fervent prayer of a righteous man availeth much.*

D. We may be in health even as our soul prospereth.

III John 2, *Beloved, I wish above all things that thou mayest prosper and be in health, even as thy soul prospereth.*

E. Healing comes by partaking of the Lord's Supper.

I Corinthians 11:29-30, *For he that eateth and drinketh unworthily, eateth and drinketh damnation to himself, not discerning the Lord's body.*
v. 30, *For this cause many are weak and sickly among you, and many sleep.*

NOTES

STUDY GUIDE

INDIANA CHRISTIAN UNIVERSITY

CHRISTIAN FOUNDATIONS

Lesson 13

WHY WE BELIEVE IN
THE SECOND COMING OF CHRIST

INTRODUCTION:

The second coming of Christ is mentioned more than 300 times in the New Testament. Paul refers to it in his epistles at least 50 times. Whole books (I and II Thessalonians) and chapters (Matthew 24; Mark 13) are devoted to it. It is, without doubt, one of the most important doctrines of the New Testament; therefore, we believe He is coming again. The Second Coming is divided into two events: the Rapture (when all Christians shall be caught up to meet the Lord in the air) and the Revelation (when the Lord comes back to earth with the saints to set up His Kingdom). This lesson is concerned with the Rapture.

READING:

I Thessalonians 4:13, 16-17, *But I would not have you to be ignorant, brethren, concerning them which are asleep, that ye sorrow not, even as others which have no hope.*

v. 16, *For the Lord himself shall descend from heaven with a shout, with the voice of the archangel, and with the trump of God: and the dead in Christ shall rise first:*
v. 17, *Then we which are alive and remain shall be caught up together with them in the clouds to meet the Lord in the air: and so shall we ever be with the Lord.*

1. THE SIGNS OF HIS COMING

    A. The sign of the days of Noah and Lot

        1) Matthew 24:37-39, *But as the days of Noe were, so shall also the coming of the Son of man be.*
            v. 38, *For as in the days that were before the flood they were eating and drinking, marrying and giving in marriage, until the day that Noe entered into the ark,*
            v. 39, *And knew not until the flood came, and took them all away; so shall also the coming of the Son of man be.*

2)   Luke 17:26-30, *And as it was in the days of Noe, so shall it be also in the days of the Son of man.*
v. 27, They did eat, they drank, they married wives, they were given in marriage, until the day that Noe entered into the ark, and the flood came, and destroyed them all.
v. 28, Likewise also as it was in the days of Lot; they did eat, they drank, they bought, they sold, they planted, they builded;
v. 29, But the same day that Lot went out of Sodom it rained fire and brinstone from heaven, and destroyed them all.
v. 30, Even thus shall it be in the day when the Son of man is revealed.

B.   The sign of world evangelization

Matthew 24:14, *And this gospel of the kingdom shall be preached in all the world for a witness unto all nations; and then shall the end come.*

C.   The budding of the fig tree: the Jews return to the Holy Land

Luke 21:24, 29-30, *And they shall fall by the edge of the sword, and shall be led away captive into all nations: and Jerusalem shall be trodden down of the Gentiles, until the times of the Gentiles be fulfilled.*

v. 29, And he spake to them a parable; Behold the fig tree, and all the trees;
v. 30, When they now shoot forth, ye see and knwo of your own selves that summer is not nigh at hand.

D.   The sign of the generation which shall see these things

Matthew 24:34, . . .*This generation shall not pass, till all things be fulfilled.*

E.   Wars, economic disturbances, persecution

Matthew 24:6-13, *And ye shall hear of wars and rumours of wars: see that ye be not troubled: for all these things must come to pass, but the end is not yet.*
v. 7, For nation shall rise against nation, and kingdom against kingdom: and there shall be famines, and pestilences, and earthquakes, in divers places.
v. 8, All these are the beginning of sorrows.
v. 9, Then shall they deliver you up to be afflicted, and shall kill you: and ye shall be hated of all nations for my name's sake.
v. 10, And then shall many be offended, and shall betray one another, and shall hate one another.
v. 11, And many false prophets shall rise, and shall deceive many.
v. 12, And because iniquity shall abound, the love of many shall wax cold.
v. 13, But he that shall endure unto the end, the same shall be saved.

2.   THE MANNER OF HIS COMING

A.   He will come in person.

1)   Acts 1:11, *Which also said, Ye men of Galilee, why stand ye gazing up into heaven? this same Jesus, which is taken up from you into heaven, shall so come in like manner as ye have seen him go into heaven.*

2)   John 14:3, *And if I go and prepare a place for you, I will come again, and receive you unto myself; that where I am, there ye may be also.*

B.   His coming will be glorious. He will come with a shout, with the voice of the archangel, and the trump of God. The dead in Christ will rise from graves. They, along with the living Christians, will be caught up to meet the Lord in the air. We shall be changed into His likeness.

   1)   I Thessalonians 4:16, *For the Lord himself shall descend from heaven with a shout, with the voice of the archangel, and with the trump of God: and the dead in Christ shall rise first:*

   2)   Colossians 3:4, *When Christ, who is our life, shall appear, then shall ye also appear with him in glory.*

   3)   Philippians 3:20-21, *For our conversation is in heaven; from whence also we look for the Saviour, the Lord Jesus Christ:*
   v. 21, *Who shall change our vile body, that it may be fashioned like unto his glorious body, according to the working whereby he is able even to subdue all things unto himself.*

   4)   I John 3:2, *Beloved, now are we the sons of God, and doth not yet appear what we shall be: but we know that, when he shall appear, we shall be like him; for we shall see him as he is.*

C.   He will come in the clouds.

   Revelation 1:7, *Behold, he cometh with clouds; and every eye shall see him, and they also which pierced him: and all kindreds of the earth shall wail because of him. Even so, Amen.*

D.   One shall be taken, another left.

Luke 17:34-36, *I tell you, in that night there shall be two men in one bed; the one shall be taken, and the other shall be left.*
v. 35, *Two women shall be grinding together; the one Shall be taken, and the other left.*
v. 36, *Two men shall be in the field; the one shall be taken, and the other left.*

3.   THE TIME OF HIS COMING

A.   The day and hour is not known by any man.

Matthew 24:36, 42, *But of that day and hour knoweth no man, no, not the angels of heaven, but my Father only.*

v. 42, *Watch therefore: for ye know not what hour your Lord doth come.*

Matthew 25:13, *Watch therefore, for ye know neither the day nor the hour wherein the Son of man cometh.*

B.   Why His coming is delayed

1)   James 5:7, *Be patient therefore, brethren, unto the coming of the Lord. Behold, the husbandman waiteth for the precious fruit of the earth, and hath long patience for it, until he receive the early and latter rain.*

2)   II Peter 3:9, *The Lord is not slack concerning his promise, as some men count slackness; but is longsuffering to us-ward, not willing that any should perish, but that all should come to repentance.*

3)   Our attitude

James 5:8, *Be ye also patient; stablish your hearts: for the coming of the Lord draweth nigh.*

C.   His coming will be in the twinkling of an eye.

I Corinthians 15:51-52, *Behold, I shew you a mystery; We shall not all sleep, but we shall all be changed.*
v. 52, *In a moment, in the twinkling of an eye, at the last trump: for the trumpet shall sound, and the dead shall be raised incorruptible, and we shall be changed.*

4. THE PURPOSE OF HIS COMING

   A. To catch His bride away from the Great Tribulation

     1) I Thessalonians 5:9, *For God hath not appointed us to wrath, but to obtain salvation by our Lord Jesus Christ.*

     2) Matthew 24:21, *For then shall be great tribulation, such as was not since the beginning of the world to this time, no, nor ever shall be.*

     3) Mark 13:19, *For in those days shall be affliction, such as was not from the beginning of the creation which God created unto this time, neither shall be.*

   B. To reward every man according to his works

     1) II Corinthians 5:10, *For we must all appear before the judgment seat of Christ; that every one may receive the things done in his body, according to that he hath done, whether it be good or bad.*

     2) Revelation 22:12, *And, behold, I come quickly; and my reward is with me, to give every man according as his work shall be.*

   C. To take us to the home He has prepared

   John 14:3, *And if I go and prepare a place for you, I will come again, and receive you unto myself; that where I am, there ye may be also.*

5. THOSE LEFT AFTER THE RAPTURE

   A. Will go through the Great Tribulation

   Luke 21:34-36, *And take heed to yourselves, lest at any time your hearts be overcharged with surfeiting, and drunkenness, and cares of this life, and so that day come upon you unawares.*
   v. 35, *For as a snare shall it come on all them that dwell on the face of the whole earth.*
   v. 36, *Watch ye therefore, and pray always, that ye may be accounted worthy to escape all these things that shall come to pass, and to stand before the Son of man.*

B.   Will not be able to buy or sell without the mark of the beast

Revelation 13:16-17, *And he causeth all, both small and great, rich and poor, free and bond, to receive a mark in their right hand, or in their foreheads:*
v. 17, And that no man might buy or sell, save he that had the mark, or the name of the beast, or the number of his name.

C.   Will have to give up their lives to be saved

Revelation 6:9, *And when he had opened the fifth seal, I saw under the altar the souls of them that were slain for the word of God, and for the testimony which they held.*

Revelation 20:4, *And I saw thrones, and they sat upon them, and judgment was given unto them: and I saw the souls of them that were beheaded for the witness of Jesus, and for the word of God, and which had not worshipped the beast, neither his image, neither had received his mark upon their foreheads, or in their hands; and they lived and reigned with Christ a thousand years.*

6.   PARABLES OF THE SECOND COMING

A.   Faithful and unfaithful servant

Matthew 24:45-51, *Who then is a faithful and wise servant, whom his lord hath made ruler over his household, to give them meat in due season?*
v. 46, Blessed is that servant, whom his lord when he cometh shall find so doing.
v. 47, Verily I say unto you, That he shall make him ruler over all his goods.
v. 48, But if that evil servant shall say in his heart, My lord delayeth his coming;
v. 49, And shall begin to smite his fellowservants, and to eat and drink with the drunken;
v. 50, The lord of that servant shall come in a day when he looketh not for him, and in an hour that he is not aware of,
v. 51, And shall cut him asunder, and appoint him his portion with the hypocrites: there shall be weeping and gnashing of teeth.

B. The man on a far journey

Mark 13:34-37, *For the Son of man is as a man taking a far journey, who left his house, and gave authority to his servants, and to every man his work, and commanded the porter to watch.*
v. 35, *Watch ye therefore: for ye know not when the master of the house cometh, at even, or at midnight, or at the cockcrowing, or in the morning:*
v. 36, *Lest coming suddenly he find you sleeping.*
v. 37, *And what I say unto you I say unto all, Watch.*

C. The ten virgins

Matthew 25:1, 6-10, *Then shall the kingdom of heaven be likened unto ten virgins, which took their lamps, and went forth to meet the bridegroom.*

v. 6, *And at midnight there was a cry made, Behold, the bridegroom cometh; go ye out to meet him.*
v. 7, *Then all those virgins arose, and trimmed their lamps.*
v. 8, *And the foolish said unto the wise, Give us of your oil; for our lamps are gone out.*
v. 9, *But the wise answered, saying, Not so; lest there be not enough for us and you: but go ye rather to them that sell, and buy for yourselves.*
v. 10, *And while they went to buy, the bridegroom came; and they that were ready went in with him to the marriage: and the door was shut.*

D. The talents

Matthew 25:14-19, 29-30, *For the kingdom of heaven is as a man travelling into a far country, who called his own servants, and delivered unto them his goods.*
v. 15, *And unto one he gave five talents, to another two, and to another one; to every man according to his several ability; and straightway took his journey.*
v. 16, *Then he that had received the five talents went and traded with the same, and made them other five talents.*
v. 17, *And likewise he that had received two, he also gained other two.*
v. 18, *But he that had received one went and digged in the earth, and hid his lord's money.*
v. 19, *After a long time the lord of those servants cometh, and reckoneth with them.*

v. 29, *For unto every one that hath shall be given, and he shall have abundance: but from him that hath not shall be taken away even that which he hath.*
v. 30, *And cast ye the unprofitable servant into outer darkness: there shall be weeping and gnashing of teeth.*

E.   The pounds

Luke 19:12-15, 26-27, *He said therefore, A certain nobleman went into a far country to receive for himself a kingdom, and to return.*
v. 13, *And he called his ten servants, and delivered them ten pounds, and said unto them, Occupy till I come.*
v. 14, *But his citizens hated him, and sent a message after him, saying, We will not have this man to reign over us.*
v. 15, *And it came to pass, that when he was returned, having received the kingdom, then he commanded these servants to be called unto him, to whom he had given the money, that he might know how much every man had gained by trading.*

v. 26, *For I say unto you, That unto every one which hath shall be given; and from him that hath not, even that he hath shall be taken away from him.*
v. 27, But those mine enemies, which would not that I should reign over them, bring hither, and slay them before me.*

STUDY GUIDE

INDIANA CHRISTIAN UNIVERSITY

CHRISTIAN FOUNDATIONS

Lesson 14

WHY WE BELIEVE
JESUS IS THE SON OF GOD

INTRODUCTION:

John wrote to prove that Jesus was the Christ, the promised Messiah, and the Son of God. In Matthew and Luke, "Son of David" and "Son of God" link Christ to the earth. In John, "Son of God" connects Him with the Father in heaven that faith might be produced and eternal life might be received.

READING:

John 1:1-3, 9-14, *In the beginning was the Word, and the Word was with God, and the Word was God.*
v. 2, *The same was in the beginning with God.*
v. 3, *All things were made by him; and without him was not any thing made that was made.*

v. 9, *That was the true Light, which lighteth every man that cometh into the world.*
v. 10, *He was in the world, and the world was made by him, and the world knew him not.*
v. 11, *He came unto his own, and his own received him not.*
v. 12, *But as many as received him, to them gave he power to become the sons of God, even to them that believe on his name:*
v. 13, *Which were born, not of blood, nor of the will of the flesh, nor of the will of man, but of God.*
v. 14, *And the Word was made flesh, and dwelt among us, (and we beheld his glory, the glory as of the only begotten of the Father,) full of grace and truth.*

1. CHRIST'S LIFE DID NOT BEGIN WHEN HE WAS BORN

A. He was the Creator of the universe.

   1) John 1:3, 10, *All things were made by him; and without him was not any thing made that was made.*

   v. 10, *He was in the world, and the world was made by him, and the world knew him not.*

   2) Colossians 1:16, *For by him were all things created, that are in heaven, and that are in earth, visible and invisible, whether they be thrones, or dominions, or principalities, or powers: all things were created by him, and for him.*

B. "The Word" is His eternal name.

   1) John 1:1, *In the beginning was the Word, and the Word was with God, and the Word was God.*

   2) I John 1:1, *That which was from the beginning, which we have heard, which we have seen with our eyes, which we have looked upon, and our hands have handled, of the Word of life.*

   3) Revelation 19:13, *And he was clothed with a vesture dipped in blood: and his name is called The Word of God.*

C. He came as the "Incarnate Word."

   John 1:14, *And the Word was made flesh, and dwelt among us, (and we beheld his glory, the glory as of the only begotten of the Father,) full of grace and truth.*

D. "Only Begotten Son" tells of a new relationship through the incarnation.

   1) John 13:16, 18, *Verily, verily, I say unto you, The servant is not greater than his lord; neither he that is sent greater than he that sent him.*

   v. 18, *I speak not of you all: I know whom I have chosen: but that the scripture may be fulfilled, He that eateth bread with me hath lifted up his heel against me.*

   2) Hebrews 1:5-6, *For unto which of the angels said he at any time, Thou art my Son, this day have I begotten thee? And again, I will be to him a Father, and he shall be to me a Son?*
   v. 6, *And again, when he bringeth in the firstbegotten into the world, he saith, And let all the angels of God worship him.*

3) Psalm 2:7, *I will declare the decree: the LORD hath said unto me, Thou art my Son; this day have I begotten thee.*

4) II Samuel 7:14, *I will be his father, and he shall be my son. If he commit iniquity, I will chasten him with the rod of men, and with the stripes of the children of men:*

2. CHRIST CAME TO DECLARE THE FATHER

A. Christ could declare the Father because He had known and existed with Him before coming to Earth.

1) John 1:1-2, 18, *In the beginning was the Word, and the Word was with God, and the Word was God.*
v. 2, *The same was in the beginning with God.*

v. 18, *No man hath seen God at any time; the only begotten Son, which is in the bosom of the Father, he hath declared him.*

2) "Declare" means "to draw out of the shadows of the unknown, to be the means of revealing." "He led Him forth," that is, into full revelation.

John 14:9, *Jesus saith unto him, Have I been so long time with you, and yet hast thou not known me, Philip? he that hath seen me hath seen the Father; and how sayest thou then, Shew us the Father?*

B. He was "the image of the invisible God." He was the visible form of the invisible God.

Colossians 1:15, *Who is the image of the invisible God, the firstborn of every creature.*

C. He was the "express image" of God.

1) Hebrews 1:3, *Who being the brightness of his glory, and the express image of his person, and upholding all things by the word of his power, when he had by himself purged our sins, sat down on the right hand of the Majesty on high;*

2) The mark of divinity, and the characteristics of God were stamped upon Him. He was divine in nature and being.

Colossians 2:9, *For in him dwelleth all the fulness of the Godhead bodily.*

3.   SCRIPTURE REVEALS HIM AS THE SON OF GOD

   A.   God gave a testimony at His baptism and at His transfiguration.

      1)   Matthew 3:17, *And lo a voice from heaven, saying, This is my beloved Son, in whom I am well pleased.*

      2)   Matthew 17:5, *While he yet spake, behold, a bright cloud overshadowed them: and behold a voice out of the cloud, which said, This is my beloved Son, in whom I am well pleased; hear ye him.*

   B.   Jesus gave testimony to Himself.

      1)   Luke 22:70, *Then said they all, Art thou then the Son of God? And he said unto them, Ye say that I am.*

      2)   John 10:30, *I and my Father are one.*

   C.   The apostles gave testimony.

      Matthew 16:16, *And Simon Peter answered and said, Thou art the Christ, the Son of the living God.*

4.   CHRIST DECLARED HIMSELF TO BE THE SON OF GOD

   A.   He called Himself the Eternal One.

      John 8:58, *. . .Verily, verily, I say unto you, Before Abraham was, I am.*

   B.   He called Himself the Messiah.

      John 4:25-26, *The woman saith unto him, I know that Messiah cometh, which is called Christ: when he is come, he will tell us all things.*
      v. 26, *Jesus saith unto her, I that speak unto thee am he.*

   C.   He said He was from above.

      John 8:23, *And he said unto them, Ye are from beneath; I am from above: ye are of this world; I am not of this world.*

   D.   He admitted that He was Lord and Master.

      John 13:13, *Ye call me Master and Lord: and ye say well; for so I am.*

5.   HE WAS DECLARED THE SON OF GOD BY MIGHTY MIRACLES

A.   He turned the water into wine.

John 2:9-11, *When the ruler of the feast had tasted the water that was made wine, and knew not whence it was: (but the servants which drew the water knew;) the governor of the feast called the bridegroom,*
v. 10, *And saith unto him, Every man at the beginning doth set forth good wine; and when men have well drunk, then that which is worse: but thou hast kept the good wine until now.*
v. 11, *This beginning of miracles did Jesus in Cana of Galilee, and manifested forth his glory; and his disciples believed on him.*

B.   He fed the 5,000.

John 6:9-14, *There is a lad here, which hath five barley loaves, and two small fishes: but what are they among so many?*
v. 10, *And Jesus said, Make the men sit down. Now there was much grass in the place. So the men sat down, in number about five thousand.*
v. 11, *And Jesus took the loaves; and when he had given thanks, he distributed to the disciples, and the disciples to them that were set down; and likewise of the fishes as much as they would.*
v. 12, *When they were filled, he said unto his disciples, Gather up the fragments that remain, that nothing be lost.*
v. 13, *Therefore they gathered them together, and filled twelve baskets with the fragments of the five barley loaves, which remained over and above unto them that had eaten.*
v. 14, *Then those men, when they had seen the miracle that Jesus did, said, This is of a truth that prophet that should come into the world.*

C.   He walked on the water.

John 6:19-21, *So when they had rowed about five and twenty or thirty furlongs, they see Jesus walking on the sea, and drawing nigh unto the ship: and they were afraid.*
v. 20, *But he saith unto them, It is I; be not afraid.*
v. 21, *Then they willingly received him into the ship: and immediately the ship was at the land whither they went.*

D.   He raised Lazarus from the dead.

John 11:43-45, *And when he thus had spoken, he cried with a loud voice, Lazarus, come forth.*
v. 44, *And he that was dead came forth, bound hand and foot with graveclothes: and his face was bound about with a napkin. Jesus saith unto them, Loose him, and let him go.*
v. 45, *Then many of the Jews which came to Mary, and had seen the things which Jesus did, believed on him.*

6.   "LORD JESUS CHRIST" IS HIS FULL NEW TESTAMENT NAME

A.   "Lord" is the name of His deity.

B.   "Jesus" is the name of His humanity.

1)   Matthew 1:21, *And she shall bring forth a son, and thou shalt call his name JESUS: for he shall save his people from their sins.*

2)   Luke 1:31, *And, behold, thou shalt conceive in thy womb, and bring forth a son, and shalt call his name JESUS.*

C.   "Christ" is the name of His office. Christ (Greek) and Messiah (Hebrew) meaning "Anointed One."

CONCLUSION:

Christ came into and not out of humanity. There was a time when He was not the son of Mary and Joseph. He lived on earth for only 33 years and in those few years made it possible for us to become the sons of God and heirs of the promises of God.

A.   John 1:12, *But as many as received him, to them gave he power to become the sons of God, even to them that believe on his name.*

B.   Romans 8:17, *And if children, then heirs; heirs of God, and joint-heirs with Christ; if so be that we suffer with him, that we may be also glorified together.*

STUDY GUIDE

INDIANA CHRISTIAN UNIVERSITY

CHRISTIAN FOUNDATIONS

Lesson 15

WHY WE BELIEVE
THE BIBLE IS THE WORD OF GOD

INTRODUCTION:

We believe in a wonderful God. We can see the evidence of God in all creation. The scientists of our world read the books of nature, but few are led to God thereby. The Christian reads directly from the Word of God and here he finds the secrets God desires to share with him, that he may find the way of truth and salvation. This is because God gave the Bible for that very purpose.

READING:

II Timothy 3:14-17, *But continue thou in the things which thou hast learned and hast been assured of, knowing of whom thou hast learned them;*
v. 15, *And that from a child thou hast known the holy scriptures, which are able to make thee wise unto salvation through faith which is in Christ Jesus.*
v. 16, *All scripture is given by inspiration of God, and profitable for doctrine, for reproof, for correction, for instruction in righteousness:*
v. 17, *That the man of God may be perfect, thoroughly furnished unto all good works.*

Psalm 119:97-99, 103, *O how love I thy law! it is my meditation all the day.*
v. 98, *Thou through thy commandments hast made me wiser than mine enemies: for they are ever with me.*
v. 99, *I have more understanding than all my teachers: for thy testimonies are my meditation.*

v. 103, *How sweet are thy words unto my taste! yea, sweeter than honey to my mouth!*

1.   HOW WE GOT OUR BIBLE

   A.   It came from God.

      II Timothy 3:16, *All scripture is given by inspiration of God, and is profitable for doctrine, for reproof, for correction, for instruction in righteousness:*

   B.   The Holy Spirit guarded truth from error.

      John 16:13, *Howbeit when he, the Spirit of truth, is come, he will guide you into all truth: for he shall not speak of himself; but whatsoever he shall hear, that shall he speak: and he will shew you things to come.*

   C.   Holy men of God recorded the Word.

      II Peter 1:21, *For the prophecy came not in old time by the will of man: but holy men of God spake as they were moved by the Holy Ghost.*

2.   HISTORY OF THE WRITING

   A.   It covers a period of 1,600 years.

   B.   It was written by 40 different men from all walks of life (kings, statesmen, prophets, priests, fishermen, shepherds, laborers).

   C.   Even though forty different personalities are evidenced in writings, there are no contradictions.

3.   BIBLE INSPIRATION DEFINED

   A.   What Bible inspiration is not:

      1)   Human inspiration or ecstasy
      2)   Human genius or ability
      3)   Verbal dictation

   B.   What Bible inspiration is:

      II Timothy 3:16, *All scripture is given by inspiration of God, and is profitable for doctrine, for reproof, for correction, for instruction in righteousness:*

      1)   Filled with the breath of God
      2)   The in-breathing of God by the Holy Spirit into men qualifying them to receive and record divine truth

4.   PROOF THAT THE BIBLE IS THE WORD OF GOD

Bible prophecies have been fulfilled in perfect and amazing detail. Some examples include:

A.   The birth of Christ

Genesis 3:15, *And I will put enmity between thee and the woman, and between thy seed and her seed; it shall bruise thy head, and thou shalt bruise his heel.*

B.   The death of Christ

Isaiah 53:1-12, *Who hath believed our report? and to whom is the arm of the LORD revealed?*
v. 2, *For he shall grow up before him as a tender plant, and as a root out of a dry ground: he hath no form nor comeliness; and when we shall see him, there is no beauty that we should desire him.*
v. 3, *He is despised and rejected of men; a man of sorrows: yet we did esteem him stricken, smitten of God and afflicted.*
v. 4, *Surely he hath borne our griefs, and carried our sorrows: yet we did esteem him stricken, smitten of God, and afflicted.*
v. 5, *But he was wounded for our transgressions, he was bruised for our iniquities: the chastisement of our peace was upon him; and with his stripes we are healed.*
v. 6, *All we like sheep have gone astray; we have turned every one to his own way; and the LORD hath laid on him the iniquity of us all.*
v. 7, *He was oppressed, and he was afflicted, yet he opened not his mouth: he is brought as a lamb to the slaughter, and as a sheep before her shearers is dumb, so he openeth not his mouth.*
v. 8, *He was taken from prison and from judgment: and who shall declare his generation? for he was cut off out of the land of the living: for the transgression of my people was he stricken.*
v. 9, *And he made his grave with the wicked, and with the rich in his death; because he had done no violence, neither was any deceit in his mouth.*
v. 10, *Yet it pleased the LORD to bruise him; he hath put him to grief: when thou shalt make his soul an offering for sin, he shall see his seed, he shall prolong his days, and the pleasure of the LORD shall prosper in his hand.*
v. 11, *He shall see of the travail of his soul, and shall be satisfied: by his knowledge shall my righteous servant justify many; for he shall bear their iniquities.*
v. 12, *Therefore will I divide him a portion with the great, and he shall divide the spoil with the strong; because he hath poured out his soul unto death: and he was numbered with the transgressors; and he bare the sin of many, and made intercession for the transgressors.*

C.   The resurrection of Christ

John 2:19-21, *Jesus answered and said unto them, Destroy this temple, and in three days I will raise it up.*
v. 20, *Then said the Jews, Forty and six years was this temple in building, and wilt thou rear it up in three days?*
v. 21, *But he spake of the temple of his body.*

D.   The giving of the Holy Spirit

Joel 2:28, *And it shall come to pass afterward, that I will pour out my spirit upon all flesh; and your sons and your daughters shall prophesy, your old men shall dream dreams, your young men shall see visions.*

5. THE POWER OF THE BIBLE BREAKS THE POWER OF SIN AND DEATH

Romans 1:16, *For I am not ashamed of the gospel of Christ: for it is the power of God unto salvation to every one that believeth; to the Jew first, and also to the Greek.*

6. THE BIBLE CANNOT BE DESTROYED

Matthew 5:18, *For verily I say unto you, Till heaven and earth pass, one jot or one tittle in no wise pass from the law, till all be fulfilled.*

7. WHAT THE BIBLE MEANS TO LOST HUMANITY

A.   It reveals the origin, state, and destiny of man.

Genesis 1:26, *And God said, Let us make man in our image, after our likeness: and let them have dominion over the fish of the sea, and over the fowl of the air, and over the cattle, and over all the earth, and over every creeping thing that creepeth upon the earth.*

B.   It reveals God's provision for all men to come to repentance.

1)   John 3:16, *For God so loved the world, that he gave his only begotten Son, that whosoever believeth in him should not perish, but have everlasting life.*

2)   II Peter 3:9, *The Lord is not slack concerning his promise, as some men count slackness; but is longsuffering to us-ward, not willing that any should perish, but that all should come to repentance.*

C.   It reveals privileges of sonship through believing upon Christ Jesus.

John 1:12, *But as many as received him, to them gave he power to become the sons of God, even to them that believe on his name.*

D.   It reveals that believers will share the glories of heaven.

1)   John 14:1-3, *Let not your heart be troubled: ye believe in God believe also in me.*
v. 2, In my Father's house are many mansions: if it were not so, I would have told you. I go to prepare a place for you.
v. 3, And if I go and prepare a place for you, I will come again, and receive you unto myself; that where I am, there ye may be also.

2)   Romans 8:17, *And if children, then heirs; heirs of God, and joint-heirs with Christ; if so be that we suffer with him, that we may be also glorified together.*

NOTES

_____

_____

_____

_____

_____

_____

_____

_____

_____

_____

_____

_____

_____

_____

_____

_____

_____

_____

_____

_____

_____

_____

_____

_____

STUDY GUIDE

INDIANA CHRISTIAN UNIVERSITY

CHRISTIAN FOUNDATIONS

Lesson 16

WHY WE BELIEVE
IN WATER BAPTISM

INTRODUCTION:

Water baptism is one of the two God-given ordinances of the church. The importance of baptism is made very clear in the Bible. Our Lord's Commission to *teach all nations* and *preach the gospel to every creature* includes *baptizing them in the name of the Father, and of the Son and of the Holy Ghost* (Matthew 28:19), and promises *he that believeth and is baptized shall be saved; but he that believeth not shall be damned* (Mark 16:16). Water baptism is an outward testimony of an inward work of grace begun in the life of the believer.

READING:

Matthew 3:13-17, *Then cometh Jesus from Galilee to Jordan unto John, to be baptized of him.*
v. 14, *But John forbad him, saying, I have need to be baptized of thee, and comest thou to me?*
v. 15, *And Jesus answering said unto him, Suffer it to be so now: for thus it becometh us to fulfill all righteousness. Then he suffered him.*
v. 16, *And Jesus, when he was baptized, went up straightway out of the water: and, lo, the heavens were opened unto him, and he saw the Spirit of God descending like a dove, and lighting upon him:*
v. 17, *And lo a voice from heaven, saying, This is my beloved Son, in whom I am well pleased.*

Acts 8:36-38, *And as they went on their way, they came unto a certain water: and the eunuch said, See, here is water; what doth hinder me to be baptized?*
v. 37, *And Philip said, If thou believest with all thine heart, thou mayest. And he answered and said, I believe that Jesus Christ is the Son of God.*
v. 38, *And he commanded the chariot to stand still: and they went down both into the water, both Philip and the eunuch; and he baptized him.*

1. WHO SHOULD BE BAPTIZED?

A. Born-again believers who have repented of their sins.

    1) Mark 16:16, *He that believeth and is baptized shall be saved; but he that believeth not shall be damned.*

    2) Acts 2:38, *Then Peter said unto them, Repent, and be baptized every one of you in the name of Jesus Christ for the remission of sins, and ye shall receive the gift of the Holy Ghost.*

B. Backsliders who come back to God should do the first works again.

    1) Ezekiel 3:20, *Again, when a righteous man doth turn from his righteousness, and commit iniquity, and I lay a stumblingblock before him, he shall die: because thou hast not given him warning, he shall die in his sin, and his righteousness which he hath done shall not be remembered; but his blood will I require at thine hand.*

       Ezekiel 18:24, *But when the righteous turneth away from his righteousness, and committeth iniquity, and doeth according to all the abominations that the wicked man doeth, shall he live? All his righteousness that he hath done shall not be mentioned: in his trespass that he hath trespassed, and in his sin that he hath sinned, in them shall he die.*

       Ezekiel 33:13, *When I shall say to the righteous, that he shall surely live; if he trust to his own righteousness, and commit iniquity, all his righteousness shall he die for it.*

    2) Revelation 2:4-5, *Nevertheless I have somewhat against thee, because thou hast left thy first love.*
       v. 5, *Remember therefore from whence thou art fallen, and repent, and do the first works; or else I will come unto thee quickly, and will remove thy candlestick out of his place, except thou repent.*

C.   Babies are to be dedicated, not baptized.

1)   Luke 2:22, *And when the days of her purification according to the law of Moses were accomplished, they brought him to Jerusalem, to present him to the Lord.*

2)   Mark 10:13-16, *And they brought young children to him, that he should touch them: and his disciples rebuked those that brought them.*
v. 14, But when Jesus saw it, he was much displeased, and said unto them, Suffer the little children to come unto me, and forbid them not: for of such is the kingdom of God.
v. 15, Verily I say unto you, Whosoever shall not receive the kingdom of God as a little child, he shall not enter therein.
v. 16, And he took them up in his arms, put his hands upon them, and blessed them.

2.   WHY CHRISTIANS SHOULD BE BAPTIZED

A.   They are to follow the example of Jesus and fulfill all righteousness.

Matthew 3:15, *And Jesus answering said unto him, Suffer it to be so now: for thus it becometh us to fulfil all righteousness. Then he suffered him.*

B.   They are to be obedient to Christ's command.

Matthew 28:19, *Go ye therefore, and teach all nations, baptizing them in the name of the Father, and of the Son, and of the Holy Ghost.*

C.   Acts 8:37, *And Philip said, If thou believest with all thine heart, thou mayest. And he answered and said, I believe that Jesus Christ is the Son of God.*

3.   HOW CHRISTIANS SHOULD BE BAPTIZED

A.   By immersion: "Baptize" comes from the Greek word *baptidzo,* meaning "to bury." To fulfill the true sense of the word, the believer must be completely buried or immersed in water.

B.   In the name of the Father, Son, and Holy Spirit:

1)   Matthew 28:19, *Go ye therefore, and teach all nations, baptizing them in the name of the Father, and of the Son, and of the Holy Ghost:*

This shows the complete harmony of the Trinity in the work of salvation. Other scriptures do not replace the formula given here by Christ, but gives the name or authority in which you are to do everything, including baptism.

2)   Acts 2:38, *Then Peter said unto them, Repent, and be baptized every one of you in the name of Jesus Christ for the remission of sins, and ye shall receive the gift of the Holy Ghost.*

Acts 10:48, *And he commanded them to be baptized in the name of the Lord. . .*

Acts 19:5, *When they heard this, they were baptized in the name of the Lord Jesus.*

3)   Colossians 3:17, *And whatsoever ye do in word or deed, do all in the name of the Lord Jesus, giving thanks to God and the Father by him.*

4.   THE SPIRITUAL SIGNIFICANCE OF WATER BAPTISM

A.   Going down into the water identifies us with the death and burial of Christ.

1)   Romans 6:3-4, *Know ye not, that so many of us as were baptized into Jesus Christ were baptized into his death?*
v. 4, *Therefore we are buried with him by baptism into death: that like as Christ was raised up from the dead by the glory of the Father, even so we also should walk in newness of life.*

2)   Colossians 2:12, *Buried with him in baptism, wherein also ye are risen with him through the faith of the operation of God, who hath raised him from the dead.*

B.   Coming up out of the water identifies us with the resurrection of Christ.

1)   Romans 6:4-5, 8, *Therefore we are buried with him by baptism into death: that like as Christ was raised up from the dead by the glory of the Father, even so we also should walk in newness of life.*
v. 5, *For if we have been planted together in the likeness of his death, we shall be also in the likeness of his resurrection:*

v. 8, *Now if we be dead with Christ, we believe that we shall also live with him.*

    2)   Colossians 2:12, *Buried with him in baptism, wherein also ye are risen with him through the faith of the operation of God, who hath raised him from the dead.*

C.   This identification with Christ is the secret of Christian life and victory.

    1)   Romans 6:11, *Likewise reckon ye also yourselves to be dead indeed unto sin, but alive unto God through Jesus Christ our Lord.*

    2)   Galatians 2:20, *I am crucified with Christ: nevertheless I live; yet not I, but Christ liveth in me: and the life which I now live in the flesh I live by the faith of the Son of God, who loved me, and gave himself for me.*

D.   We do not believe in "Regenerative Baptism."

When Jesus spoke of being *born of water* (John 3:5), He was not referring to water baptism, but to the natural birth which was all that Nicodemus could understand(v. 4). Jesus also referred to the natural birth when He said, *That which is born of the flesh is flesh* (v. 6). This is essentially a water birth. The fetus floats in water or fluid for nine months and then the water helps to usher that new life into the world. Being born of the Spirit (v. 5) is being born again (v. 3) literally from above or from God.

    1)   John 1:13, *Which were born, not of blood, nor of the will of the flesh, nor of the will of man, but of God.*

    2)   Acts 22:16, *And now why tarriest thou? arise, and be baptized, and wash away thy sins, calling on the name of the Lord.*

    We are not to wash away our sins by being baptized, but by *calling on the name of the Lord.*

    3)   I Peter 3:21, *The like figure whereunto even baptism doth also now save us (not the putting away of the filth of the flesh, but the answer of a good conscience toward God,) by the resurrection of Jesus Christ.*

    It is not "putting away the filth of the flesh" by baptism that saves us, but the answer of a good conscience toward God.

    4)   Titus 3:5, *Not by works of righteousness which we have done, but according to his mercy he saved us, by the washing of regeneration, and renewing of the Holy Ghost.*

    It is not the washing which regenerates, but the regeneration which washes.

5. TESTIMONY OF PROMINENT MEN

A. Martin Luther: "I would have those who are baptized to be entirely immersed, as the Word imparts and the mystery signifies."

B. George Whitefield: "It is certain that in the words of our text, there is a reference to the manner of baptism which is by immersion."

C. John Wesley: "I was not only immersed myself, but practiced immersion."

STUDY GUIDE

INDIANA CHRISTIAN UNIVERSITY

CHRISTIAN FOUNDATIONS

Lesson 17

WHY WE BELIEVE IN THE LORD'S SUPPER OR HOLY COMMUNION

INTRODUCTION:

There are two great ordinances set in the church, and only two--baptism and the Lord's Supper. They do not come from men but are by divine appointment. The deep meanings of Christianity are symbolized by these ordinances. This lesson is given to one of these-- "The Lord's Supper." God has had two churches--one in the Old Testament and one in the New. He has worked with both under covenants of the blood and both covenants run parallel--therefore we believe.

READING:

Matthew 26:26-28, *And as they were eating, Jesus took bread, and blessed it, and brake it, and gave it to the disciples, and said, take, eat; this is my body.*
v. 27, *And he took the cup, and gave thanks, and gave it to them, saying, Drink ye all of it;*
v. 28, *For this is my blood of the new testament, which is shed for many for the remission of sins.*

I Corinthians 11:23-25, *For I have received of the Lord that which also I delivered unto you, That the Lord Jesus the same night in which he was betrayed took bread:*
v. 24, *And when he had given thanks, he brake it, and said, Take, eat: this is my body, which is broken for you: this do in remembrance of me.*
v. 25, *After the same manner also he took the cup, when he had supped, saying, This cup is the new testament in my blood: this do ye, as oft as ye drink it, in remembrance of me.*

1. **THE OLD COVENANT (THE PASSOVER) WAS GIVEN BY GOD TO ISRAEL**

    A. The symbols of her covenant were blood sprinkled on the lintels and doorposts to keep the death angel away from the firstborn.

    Exodus 12:7, *And they shall take of the blood, and strike it on the two side posts and on the upper door post of the houses, wherein they shall eat it.*

    B. The applied blood of the lamb saved them.

    Exodus 12:13, *And the blood shall be to you for a token upon the houses where ye are: and when I see the blood, I will pass over you, and the plague shall not be upon you to destroy you, when I smite the land of Egypt.*

    C. They ate the lamb for strength for the journey.

    Exodus 12:8, *And they shall eat the flesh in that night, roast with fire, and unleavened bread; and with bitter herbs they shall eat it.*

    D. The flesh of the lamb healed them. None of their three million people were sick or weakly.

    Psalm 105:37, *He brought them forth also with silver and gold: and there was not one feeble person among their tribes.*

2. **THE NEW COVENANT WAS GIVEN BY CHRIST TO HIS DISCIPLES**

    A. One of the symbols of the New Covenant is wine, which is a type of His blood.

    I Corinthians 11:25, *After the same manner also he took the cup, when he had supped, saying, This cup is the new testament in my blood: this do ye, as oft as ye drink it, in remembrance of me.*

    B. His blood was shed for the remission of sins.

    Matthew 26:28, *For this is my blood of the new testament, which is shed for many for the remission of sins.*

    C. The bread is a symbol of His flesh.

    Matthew 26:26, *And as they were eating, Jesus took bread, and blessed it, and brake it, and gave it to the disciples, and said, Take, eat; this is my body.*

    D.   His body was broken by stripes for the healing of your body.

        1)   I Corinthians 11:24, *And when he had given thanks, he brake it, and said, Take, eat: this is my body, which is broken your you: this do in remembrance of me.*

        2)   I Peter 2:24, *Who his own self bare our sins in his own body on the tree, that we, being dead to sins, should live unto righteousness: by whose stripes ye were healed.*

3.   THE LORD'S SUPPER TO BE RECEIVED. . .

    A.   By born-again disciples only.

    I Corinthians 11:27, *Wherefore whosoever shall eat this bread, and drink this cup of the Lord, unworthily, shall be guilty of the body and the blood of the Lord.*

    B.   In faith that it is God's complete sacrifice for us.

    I Corinthians 11:26, *For as often as ye eat this bread, and drink this cup, ye do shew the Lord's death till he come.*

    C.   With discernment--self-examination or heart searching.

    I Corinthians 11:28, *But let a man examine himself, and so let him eat of that bread, and drink of that cup.*

4.   JUDGMENT TO THOSE TAKING COMMUNION UNWORTHILY

I Corinthians 11:29, *For he that eateth and drinketh unworthily, eateth and drinketh damnation to himself, not discerning the Lord's body.*

    A.   They will become sick through disease and afflictions.

    B.   They will become weak, not knowing the cause or remedy.

    C.   Many will "sleep," or die in the prime of life.

5.   THE LORD'S SUPPER IS A TIME OF REMEMBRANCE

A.   Remember His death--the scars in His hands.

I Corinthians 11:26, *For as often as ye eat this bread, and drink this cup, ye do shew the Lord's death till he come..*

B.   Remember His benefits--salvation, healing and mercy.

Psalm 103:2-4, *Bless the LORD, O my soul, and forget not all his benefits:*
v. 3, *Who forgiveth all thine iniquities; who healeth all thy diseases;*
v. 4, *Who redeemeth thy life from distruction; who crowneth thee with lovingkindness and tender mercies;*

C.   Remember, He is coming again.

I Corinthians 11:26, . . .*ye do shew the Lord's death till he come.*

CHRISTIAN FOUNDATIONS

Lesson 18

WHY WE BELIEVE
IN WORSHIPPING ON SUNDAY
OR THE LORD'S DAY

INTRODUCTION:

Whether we should worship on the Sabbath day or the Lord's Day is a controversy as old as Christianity. We study this subject using the scriptures as our final authority. The Sabbath is the seventh day of the week or Saturday. This is the day on which God rested after the work of creation. It was set apart as a day of rest for man in the law given to Moses.

READING:

Mark 16:1, 3, *And when the sabbath was past, Mary Magdalene, and Mary the mother of James, and Salome, had bought sweet spices, that they might come and anoint him.*

v. 3, *And very early in the morning the first day of the week, they came unto the sepulchre at the rising of the sun.*

THE OLD COVENANT

A. Genesis 2:2-3, *And on the seventh day God ended his work which he had made; and he rested on the seventh day from all his work which he had made.*
v. 3, *And God blessed the seventh day, and sanctified it: because that in it he had rested from all his work which God created and made.*

B. Exodus 20:9-11, *Six days shalt thou labour, and do all thy work:*

THE NEW COVENANT

A. The Lord's day is the first day of the week, or Sunday. In comparing the old covenant with the new, we are reminded that Jesus did not come to destroy, but to fulfill, the law.

Matthew 5:17-18, *Think not that I am come to destroy the law, or the prophets: I am not come to destroy, but to fulfil.*

[The Old Covenant]

v. 10, *But the seventh day is the sabbath of the LORD thy God: in it thou shalt not do any work, thou, nor thy son, nor thy daughter, thy manservant, nor thy maidservant, nor thy cattle, nor thy stranger that is within thy gates:*

v. 11, *For in six days the LORD made heaven and earth, the sea, and all that in them is, and rested the seventh day: wherefore the LORD blessed the sabbath day, and hallowed it.*

C. It was made at Mt. Sinai.

Exodus 19:11, 20, *And be ready against the third day: for the third day the LORD will come down in the sight of all the people upon mount Sinai.*

v. 20, *And the LORD came down upon mount Sinai, on the top of the mount: and the LORD called Moses up to the top of the mount; and Moses went up.*

Exodus 20:1, *And God spake all these words, saying.*

D. Its mediator was Moses.

Exodus 24:3-8, *And Moses came and told the people all the words of the LORD, and all the judgments: and all the people answered with one voice, and said, All the words which the LORD hath said will we do.*
v. 4, *And Moses wrote all the words of the LORD, and rose up early in the morning, and builded an altar under the hill, and twelve pillars, according to the twelve tribes of Israel.*

[The New Covenant]

v. 18, *For verily I say unto you, Till heaven and earth pass, one jot or one tittle shall in no wise pass from the law, till all be fulfilled*

B. Having fulfilled it by meeting all its demands, He became the mediator of a better covenant.

Hebrews 8:6, *But now hath he obtained a more excellent ministry, by how much also he is the mediator of a better covenant, which was established upon better promises.*

C. The old covenant has now passed away.

Hebrews 8:13, *In that he saith, A new covenant, he hath made the first old. Now that which decayeth and waxeth old is ready to vanish away.*

D. It was taught by Jesus during His three and a half years of ministry.

John 5:24, *Verily, verily, I say unto you, He that heareth my word, and believeth on him that sent me, hath everlasting life, and shall not come into condemnation; but is passed from death unto life.*

E. Its mediator is Jesus Christ.

Hebrew 8:6, *But now hath he obtained a more excellent ministry, by how much also he is the mediator of a better covenant, which was established upon better promises.*

102

[The Old Covenant]

v. 5, *And he sent young men of the children of Israel, which offered burnt offerings, and sacrificed peace offerings of oxen unto the LORD*
v. 6, *And Moses took half of the blood, and put it in basins; and half of the blood he sprinkled on the altar.*
v. 7, *And he took the book of the covenant, and read in the audience of the people: and they said, All that the LORD hath said will we do, and be obedient.*
v. 8, *And Moses took the blood, and sprinkled it on the people, and said, Behold the blood of the covenant which the LORD hath made with you concerning all these words.*

E. It was engraved on stone.

Exodus 24:12, *And the LORD said unto Moses, Come up to me into the mount, and be there: and I will give thee tables of stone, and a law, and commandments which I have written; that thou mayest teach them.*

F. It was written with the finger of God.

Exodus 31:18, *And he gave unto Moses, when he had made an end of communing with him upon mount Sinai, two tables of testimony, tables of stone, written with the finger of God.*

G. The Old Covenant was sealed with blood.

Exodus 24:7-8, *And he took the book of the covenant, and read in the audience of the people: and they said, All that the LORD hath said will we do, and be obedient.*

[The New Covenant]

Hebrew 9:15, *And for this cause he is the mediator of the new testament, that by means of death, for the redemption of the transgressions that were under*

the first testament, they which are called might receive the promise of eternal inheritance.

F. It is written on fleshly tables of the heart.

II Corinthians 3:3, *Forasmuch as ye are manifestly declared to be the epistle of Christ ministered by us, written not with ink, but with the Spirit of the living God; not in tables of stone, but in fleshy tables of the heart.*

G. It is written with the Holy Spirit.

II Corinthians 3:3, *. . .written not with ink, but with the Spirit of the living God.*

H. It was sealed with Christ's blood at Calvary.

1) Matthew 26:28, *For this is my blood of the new testament, which is shed for many for the remission of sins.*

2) Hebrews 9:12, 14, *Neither by the blood of goats and calves, but by his own blood he entered in once into the holy place, having obtained eternal redemption for us.*

<table>
<tr><td>[The Old Covenant]</td><td>[The New Covenant]</td></tr>
<tr><td>v. 8, *And Moses took the blood, and sprinkled it on the people, and said, Behold the blood of the covenant, which the LORD hath made with you concerning all these words.*</td><td>v. 14, *How much more shall the blood of Christ, who through the eternal Spirit offered himself without spot to God, purge your conscience from dead works to serve the living God?*</td></tr>
</table>

3. ACTIVITIES REQUIRED BY SABBATH WORSHIP

    A.   Do not work on the Sabbath day.

        Exodus 20:8, *Remember the sabbath day, to keep it holy.*

    B.   Gather no fuel on the Sabbath.

        Numbers 15:32-36, *And while the children of Israel were in the wilderness, they found a man that gathered sticks upon the sabbath day.*
        v. 33, *And they that found him gathering sticks brought him unto Moses and Aaron, and unto all the congregation.*
        v. 34, *And they put him in ward, because it was not declared what should be done to him.*
        v. 35, *And the LORD said unto Moses, The man shall be surely put to death: all the congregation shall stone him with stones without the camp.*
        v. 36, *And all the congregation brought him without the camp, and stoned him with stones, and he died; as the LORD commanded Moses.*

    C.   Meals must be prepared the day before.

        Exodus 16:23, *And he said unto them, This is that which the LORD hath said, To-morrow is the rest of the holy sabbath unto the LORD: bake that which ye will bake today, and seethe that ye will seethe; and that which remaineth over lay up for you to be kept until the morning.*

    D.   Kindle no fire in the home.

        Exodus 35:2-3, *Six days shall work be done, but on the seventh day there shall be to you an holy day, a sabbath of rest to the LORD: whosoever doeth work therein shall be put to death.*
        v. 3, *Ye shall kindle no fire throughout your habitations upon the sabbath day.*

4.   CHRIST'S TEACHING ABOUT THE SABBATH

A.   It is lawful to do good on the Sabbath.

Mark 3:1-5, *And he entered again into the synagogue; and there was a man there which had a withered hand.*
v. 2, *And they watched him, whether he would heal him on the sabbath day; that they might accuse him.*
v. 3, *And he saith unto the man which had the withered hand, Stand forth.*
v. 4, *And he saith unto them, Is it lawful to do good on the sabbath days, or to do evil? to save life, or to kill? But they held their peace.*
v. 5, *And when he had looked round about on them with anger, being grieved for the hardness of their hearts, he saith unto the man, Stretch forth thine hand. And he stretched it out: and his hand was restored whole as the other.*

B.   The Sabbath was made for man.

Mark 2:27, *And he said unto them, The sabbath was made for man, and not man for the sabbath.*

C.   The Son of man is Lord of the Sabbath.

Mark 2:28, *Therefore the Son of man is Lord also of the sabbath.*

5.   OUR PRIVILEGES UNDER GRACE

A.   The ceremonial law was abolished in Christ.

Ephesians 2:15, *Having abolished in his flesh the enmity, even the law of commandments contained in ordinances; for to make in himself of twain one new man, so making peace.*

B.   We have complete liberty in the Lord.

II Corinthians 3:17, *Now the Lord is that Spirit: and where the Spirit of the Lord is, there is liberty.*

C.   We are free to worship God on the day of our choosing.

Romans 14:4-6, *Who art thou that judgest another man's servant? to his own master he standeth or falleth. Yea, he shall be holden up: for God is able to make him stand.*
v. 5, *One man esteemeth one day above another: another esteemeth every day alike. Let every man be fully persuaded in his own mind.*

v. 6, *He that regardeth the day, regardeth it unto the Lord; and he that regardeth not the day, to the Lord he doth not regard it. He that eateth, eateth to the Lord, for he giveth God thanks; and he that eateth not, to the Lord he eateth not, and giveth God thanks.*

D. As the day of His appearing draws nigh, we are to increase the frequency of our assemblies.

Hebrews 10:25, *Not forsaking the assembling of ourselves together, as the manner of some is; but exhorting one another: and so much the more, as ye see the day approaching.*

6. WE WORSHIP ON THE FIRST DAY OF THE WEEK BECAUSE. . .

A. Christ rose from the dead on the first day.

Mark 16:9, *Now when Jesus was risen early the first day of the week, he appeared first to Mary Magdalene, out of whom he had cast seven devils.*

B. Christ appeared to the disciples on the first day.

John 20:19, *Then the same day at evening, being the first day of the week, when the doors were shut where the disciples were assembled for fear of the Jews, came Jesus and stood in the midst, and saith unto them, Peace be unto you.*

C. The Holy Spirit was given on the first day.

1) Acts 2:1, *And when the day of Pentecost was fully come, they were all with one accord in one place.*

2) Leviticus 23:15-16, *And ye shall count unto you from the morrow after the sabbath, from the day that ye brought the sheaf of the wave offering; seven sabbaths shall be complete:*
v. 16, *Even unto the morrow after the seventh sabbath shall ye number fifty days; and ye shall offer a new meat offering unto the LORD.*

D. Apostles and disciples broke bread on the first day.

Acts 20:7, *And upon the first day of the week, when the disciples came together to break bread, Paul preached unto them, ready to depart on the morrow; and continued his speech until midnight.*

E.   Paul commanded the people to give offerings on the first day.

I Corinthians 16:2, *Upon the first day of the week let every one of you lay by him in store, as God hath prospered him, that there be no gatherings when I come.*

F.   John worshipped on the Lord's Day.

Revelation 1:10, *I was in the Spirit on the Lord's day, and heard behind me a great voice, as of a trumpet.*

NOTES

_____

_____

_____

_____

_____

_____

_____

_____

_____

_____

_____

_____

_____

_____

_____

_____

_____

_____

_____

_____

_____

_____

_____

_____

CHRISTIAN FOUNDATIONS

Lesson 19

WHY WE BELIEVE
IN TITHING

INTRODUCTION:

Selfishness has existed almost as long as people have been on the earth and it is one of the most distasteful traits a person can have. Because God desired that His people be open-hearted and generous, He instituted the offering of sacrifices and tithing from the beginning of time. All that we possess is provided for us by God, and He asks that we return a portion of it to Him.

READING:

Malachi 3:8-12, *Will a man rob God? Yet ye have robbed me. But ye say, Wherein have we robbed thee? In tithes and offerings.*
v. 9, *Ye are cursed with a curse: for ye have robbed me, even this whole nation.*
v. 10, *Bring ye all the tithes into the store house, that there may be meat in mine house, and prove me now herewith, saith the LORD of hosts, if I will not open you the windows of heaven, and pour you out a blessing, that there shall not be room enough to receive it.*
v. 11, *And I will rebuke the devourer for your sakes, and he shall not destroy the fruits of your ground; neither shall your vine cast her fruit before the time in the field, saith the LORD of hosts.*
v. 12, *And all nations shall call you blessed: for ye shall call you blessed: for ye shall be a delightsome land, saith the LORD of hosts.*

1. GREAT MEN TITHED

    A.   Abraham tithed to Melchizedek.

        1)   Genesis 14:20-24, *And blessed be the most high God, which hath delivered thine enemies into thy hand. And he gave him tithes of all.*
                v. 21, *And the king of Sodom said unto Abram, Give me the persons, and take the goods to thyself.*

109

v. 22, *And Abram said to the king of Sodom, I have lift up mine hand unto the LORD, the most high God, the possessor of heaven and earth,*
v. 23, *That I will not take from a thread even to a shoelatchet, and that I will not take any thing that is thine, lest thou shouldest say, I have made Abram rich:*
v. 24, *Save only that which the young men have eaten, and the portion of the men which went with me, Aner, Eshcol, and Mamre; let them take their portion.*

   2)   Hebrews 7:4-6, *Now consider how great this man was, unto whom even the partriarch Abraham gave the tenth of the spoils.*
v. 5, *And verily they that are of the sons of Levi, who receive the office of the priesthood, have a commandment to take tithes of the people according to the law, that is, of their brethren, though they come out of the loins of Abraham:*
v. 6, *But he whose descent is not counted from them received tithes of Abraham, and blessed him that had the promises.*

B.   At Bethel, Jacob pledged tithes to God.

Genesis 28:22, *And this stone, which I have set for a pillar, shall be God's house: and of all that thou shalt give me I will surely give the tenth unto thee.*

C.   Moses taught the Israelites to tithe.

Leviticus 27:30-33, *And all the tithe of the land, whether of the seed of the land, or of the fruit of the tree, is the LORD's: it is holy unto the LORD.*
v. 31, *And if a man will at all redeem ought of his tithes, he shall add thereto the fifth part thereof.*
v. 32, *And concerning the tithe of the herd, or of the flock, even of whatsoever passeth under the rod, the tenth shall be holy unto the LORD.*
v. 33, *He shall not search whether it be good or bad, neither shall he change it: and if he change it at all, then both it and the change thereof shall be holy; it shall not be redeemed.*

2.   GOD'S WORD TEACHES TITHING

A.   We are commanded to give.

   1)   Proverbs 3:9, *Honour the LORD with thy substance, and with the first fruits of all thine increase:*

      2)   Malachi 3:10, *Bring ye all the tithes into the storehouse, that there may be meat in mine house, and prove me now herewith, saith the LORD of hosts, if I will not open you the windows of heaven, and pour you out a blessing, that there shall not be room enough to receive it.*

    B.   There is a judgment on those who withhold tithes.

      1)   Malachi 3:9, *Ye are cursed with a curse: for ye have robbed me, even this whole nation.*

      2)   Proverbs 11:24, *There is that scattereth, and yet increaseth; and there is that withholdeth more than is meet, but it tendeth to poverty.*

    C.   Where we invest our money, that's where our affections will be.

    Matthew 6:19-21, *Lay not up for yourselves treasures upon earth, where moth and rust doth corrupt, and where thieves break through and steal:*
v. 20, *But lay up for yourselves treasures in heaven, where neither moth nor rust doth corrupt, and where thieves do not break through nor steal:*
v. 21, *For where your treasure is, there will your heart be also.*

    D.   God loves a cheerful giver.

    II Corinthians 9:7, *Every man according as he purposeth in his heart, so let him give; not grudgingly, or of necessity: for God loveth a cheerful giver.*

    E.   Bring the tithe to the storehouse on the first day of the week.

    I Corinthians 16:2, *Upon the first day of the week let every one of you lay by him in store, as God hath prospered him, that there be no gatherings when I come.*

3.   GIVING TO GOD AND HIS WORK BRINGS BLESSING

    A.   These blessings are unlimited.

      1)   Malachi 3:10, *...prove me now herewith, saith the LORD of hosts, if I will not open you the windows of heaven, and pour you out a blessing, that there shall not be room enough to receive it.*

      2)   Proverbs 3:10, *So shall thy barns be filled with plenty, and thy presses shall burst out with new wine.*

    B.   The liberal soul shall be made fat.

         Proverbs 11:25, *The liberal soul shall be made fat: and he that watereth shall be watered also himself.*

    C.   Give and it shall be given unto you.

        1)   Luke 6:38, *Give, and it shall be given unto you; good measure, pressed down, and shaken together, and running over, shall men give into your bosom. For with the same measure that ye mete withal it shall be measured to you again.*

        2)   II Corinthians 9:6, *But this I say, He which soweth sparingly shall reap also sparingly; and he which soweth bountifully shall reap also bountifully.*

CONCLUSION:

Man's life is brief. How foolish it is for him to store treasures in a place he must soon leave. How insecure is his treasure while he is still here. Bonds may depreciate. Health may fail before a man can enjoy the wealth he slaves to obtain. Then death, the great thief, finally robs him of all his possessions with one stroke. Let us remember that only as we generously devote our means to the work of God will treasure await us in heaven.

CHRISTIAN FOUNDATIONS

Lesson 20

WHY WE BELIEVE
IN STEWARDSHIP

INTRODUCTION:

Stewardship involves one principle thought: God is the owner of all. We are stewards. Paul expressed it this way:

A. I Corinthians 6:19-20, *What? know ye not that your body is the temple of the Holy Ghost which is in you, which ye have of God, and ye are not your own?* v. 20, *For ye are bought with a price: therefore glorify God in your body, and in your spirit, which are God's.*

B. Peter describes the price

I Peter 1:19, *But with the precious blood of Christ, as of a lamb without blemish and without spot.*

More attention needs to be given to the inner spiritual springs from which the streams of true stewardship flow. We must get beyond the money question to man himself, beyond what a man gives to what he is.

READING:

Matthew 25:14-19, 29-30, *For the kingdom of heaven is as a man travelling into a far country, who called his own servants, and delivered unto them his goods.*
v. 15, *And unto one he gave five talents, to another two, and to another one; to every man according to his several ability; and straightway took his journey.*
v. 16, *Then he that had received the five talents went and traded with the same, and made them other five talents.*
v. 17, *And likewise he that had received two, he also gained other two.*
v. 18, *But he that had received one went and digged in the earth, and hid his lord's money.*
v. 19, *After a long time the lord of those servants cometh, and reckoneth with them.*

v. 29, *For unto every one that hath shall be given, and he shall have abundance: but from him that hath not shall be taken away even that which he hath.*

v. 30, *And cast ye the unprofitable servant into outer darkness: there shall be weeping and gnashing of teeth.*

1. TRUTHS TO BE REMEMBERED

A. God the maker and owner

    1) Psalm 24:1-2, *The earth is the LORD's, and the fulness thereof; the world, and they that dwell therein.*
    v. 2, *For he hath founded it upon the seas, and established it upon the floods.*

    2) Romans 14:8, *For whether we live, we live unto the Lord; and whether we die, we die unto the Lord: whether we live therefore, or die, we are the Lord's.*

B. Men are stewards, not owners.

    1) Acts 4:32, *And the multitude of them that believed were of one heart and of one soul: neither said any of them that ought of the things which he possessed was his own; but they had all things common.*

    2) I Corinthians 4:7, *For who maketh thee to differ from another? and what hast thou that thou didst not receive? now if thou didst receive it, why dost thou glory, as if thou hadst not received it?*

C. Faithfulness is required.

    1) Luke 16:1-2,10, *. . .There was a certain rich man, which had a steward; and the same was accused unto him that he had wasted his goods.*
    v. 2, *And he called him, and said unto him, How is it that I hear this of thee? give an account of thy stewardship; for thou mayest be no longer steward.*

    v. 10, *He that is faithful in that which is least is faithful also in much: and he that is unjust in the least is unjust also in much.*

    2) I Corinthians 4:2, *Moreover it is required in stewards, that a man be found faithful.*

D.   Our life is precious.

Matthew 16:26, *For what is a man profited, if he shall gain the whole world, and lose his own soul? or what shall a man give in exchange for his soul?*

E.   We must give account of our stewardship.

1)   Matthew 18:23, *Therefore is the kingdom of heaven likened unto a certain king, which would take account of his servants.*

2)   Romans 14:10, *But why dost thou judge thy brother? or why dost thou set at nought thy brother? for we shall all stand before the judgment seat of Christ.*

We have a responsibility of stewardship.

F.   Acts 5:1-5, *But a certain man named Ananias, with Sapphira his wife, sold a possession,*
v. 2, And kept back part of the price, his wife also being privy to it, and brought a certain part, and laid it at the apostles' feet.
v. 3, But Peter said, Ananias, why hath Satan filled thine heart to lie to the Holy Ghost, and keep back part of the price of the land?
v. 4, Whiles it remained, was it not thine own? and after it was sold, was it not in thine own power? why hast thou conceived this thing in thine heart? thou hast not lied unto men, but unto God.
v. 5, And Ananias hearing these words fell down, and gave up the ghost: and great fear came on all them that heard these things.

2.   LIFE'S TRUSTS TO BE HONORED

A.   Our bodies

I Corinthians 6:19-20, *What? know ye not that your body is the temple of the Holy Ghost which is in you, which ye have of God, and ye are not your own?*
v. 20, For ye are bought with a price: therefore glorify God in your body, and in your spirit, which are God's.

B.   Our time

Ephesians 5:16, *Redeeming the time, because the days are evil.*

C.   Our abilities

Matthew 25:15, *And unto one he gave five talents, to another two, and to another one; to every man according to his several ability; and straightway took his journey.*

D.   Witnessing (fruit bearing)

1)   Luke 13:6-9, *He spake also this parable; A certain man had a fig tree planted in his vineyard; and he came and sought fruit theron, and found none.*
v. 7, Then said he unto the dresser of his vineyard, Behold, these three years I come seeking fruit on this fig tree, and find none: cut it down; why combereth it the ground?
v. 8, And he answering said unto him, Lord, let it alone this year also, till I shall dig about it, and dung it:
v. 9, And if it bear fruit, well: and if not, then after that thou shalt cut it down.

2)   John 15:5, 8, *I am the vine, ye are the branches: He that abideth in me, and I in him, the same bringeth forth much fruit: for without me ye can do nothing.*
v. 8, Herein is my Father glorified, that ye bear much fruit; so shall ye be my disciples.

E.   Good works

1)   Matthew 25:34-36, *Then shall the King say unto them on his right hand, Come, ye blessed of my Father, inherit the kingdom prepared for you from the foundation of the world:*
v. 35, For I was an hungred, and ye gave me meat: I was thirst, and ye gave me drink: I was a stranger, and ye took me in:
v. 36, Naked, and ye clothed me: I was sick, and ye visited me: I was in prison, and ye came unto me.

2)   Luke 10:30-33, *And Jesus answering said, A certain man went down from Jerusalem to Jericho, and fell among thieves, which stripped him of his raiment, and wounded him, and departed, leaving him half dead.*
v. 31, And by chance there came down a certain priest that way: and when he saw him, he passed by on the other side.
v. 32, And likewise a Levite, when he was at the place, came and looked on him, and passed by on the other side.
v. 33, But a certain Samaritan, as he journeyed, came where he was: and when he saw him, he had compassion on him, . . .

3) Ephesians 2:10, *For we are his workmanship, created in Christ Jesus unto good works, which God hath before ordained that we should walk in them.*

3. EXAMPLES OF STEWARDS

A. Paul (yielded life)

Galatians 2:20, *I am crucified with Christ: nevertheless I live; yet not I, but Christ liveth in me: and the life which I now live in the flesh I live by the faith of the Son of God, who loved me, and gave himself for me.*

B. Moses (a lifetime dedicated to God)

Acts 7:22-23, 29-30, 35-36, *And Moses was learned in all the wisdom of the Egyptians, and was mighty in words and in deeds.*
v. 23, *And when he was full forty years old, it came into his heart to visit his brethren the children of Israel.*

v. 29, *Then fled Moses at this saying, and was a stranger in the land of Madian, where he begat two sons.*
v. 30, *And when forty years were expired, there appeared to him in the wilderness of mount Sina an angel of the Lord in a flame of fire in a bush.*

v. 35, *This Moses whom they refused, saying, Who made thee a ruler and a judge? the same did God send to be a ruler and a deliverer by the hand of the angel which appeared to him in the bush.*
v. 36, *He brought them out, after that he had shewed wonders and signs in the land of Egypt, and in the Red sea, and in the wilderness forty years.*

C. David (abilities dedicated to God)

1) I Samuel 16:11, 21, 23, *And Samuel said unto Jesse, Are here all thy children? And he said, There remaineth yet the youngest, and, behold, he keepeth the sheep. And Samuel said unto Jesse, Send and fetch him: for we will not sit down till he come hither.*

v. 21, *And David came to Saul, and stood before him: and he loved him greatly; and he became his armour-bearer.*

v. 23, *And it came to pass, when the evil spirit from God was upon Saul, that David took an harp, and played with his hand: so Saul was refreshed, and was well, and the evil spirit departed from him.*

2) I Samuel 17:24, 35-36, 48-51, *And all the men of Israel, when they saw the man, fled from him, and were sore afraid.*

v. 35, *And I went out after him, and smote him, and delivered it out of his mouth: and when he arose against me, I caught him by his beard, and smote him, and slew him.*

v. 36, *Thy servant slew both the lion and the bear: and this uncircumcised Philistine shall be as one of them, seeing he hath defied the armies of the living God.*

v. 48, *And it came to pass, when the Philistine arose, and came and drew nigh to meet David, that David hasted, and ran toward the army to meet the Philistine.*

v. 49, *And David put his hand in his bag, and took thence a stone, and slang it, and smote the Philistine in his forehead, that the stone sunk into his forehead; and he fell upon his face to the earth.*

v. 50, *So David prevailed over the Philistine with a sling and with a stone, and smote the Philistine, and slew him; but there was no sword in the hand of David.*

v. 51, *Therefore David ran, and stood upon the Philistine, and took his sword, and drew it out of the sheath thereof, and slew him, and cut off his head therewith. And when the Philistines saw their champion was dead, they fled.*

D. Peter (great soul-winner)

1) Acts 2:40-41, *And with many other words did he testify and exhort, saying, Save yourselves from this untoward generation.*
v. 41, *Then they that gladly received his word were baptized: and the same day there were added unto them about three thousand souls.*

2) Acts 4:4, *Howbeit many of them which heard the word believed; and the number of the men was about five thousand.*

E. Dorcas (noted for her good works)

Acts 9:39, *Then Peter arose and went with them. When he was come, they brought him into the upper chamber: and all the widows stood by him weeping, and shewing the coats and garments which Dorcas made, while she was with them.*

CONCLUSION:

Stewardship is not easy. It calls for the utmost of self and service: service with joy. . .
service done as unto the Lord. No corner of one's life is exempt from it. God has always
demanded our all, and without complete surrender in all phases of our living, we will not
have a victorious life.

NOTES

_____
_____
_____
_____
_____
_____
_____
_____
_____
_____
_____
_____
_____
_____
_____
_____
_____
_____
_____
_____
_____
_____
_____
_____
_____
_____

CHRISTIAN FOUNDATIONS

Lesson 21

WHY WE BELIEVE
IN WITNESSING

INTRODUCTION:

Let's study the first parables of instruction to believers. "The candle" signifies the Christian's testimony shining in a darkened world. "The Good Samaritan" shows who our neighbor is and what our attitude should be toward them.

READING:

Matthew 5:14-16, *Ye are the light of the world. A city that is set on a hill cannot be hid.*
v. 15, *Neither do men light a candle, and put it under a bushel, but on a candlestick; and it giveth light unto all that are in the house.*
v. 16, *Let your light so shine before men, that they may see your good works, and glorify your Father which is in heaven.*

1.   THE CANDLE

    A.   Matthew 5:14, *Ye are the light of the world. A city that is set on an hill cannot be hid.*

    B.   Mark 4:21, *And he said unto them, Is a candle brought to be put under a bushel, or under a bed? and not to be set on a candlestick?*

    C.   Luke 8:16, *No man, when he hath lighted a candle, covereth it with a vessel, or putteth it under a bed; but setteth it on a candlestick, that they which enter in may see the light.*

D. The parable explained:

1) Candle--a man

Proverbs 20:27, *The spirit of man is the candle of the LORD, searching all the inward parts of the belly.*

I Corinthians 2:11, *For what man knoweth the things of a man, save the spirit of man which is in him? even so the things of God knoweth no man, but the Spirit of God.*

2) Light--a man's testimony

Psalm 18:28, *For thou wilt light my candle: the LORD my God will enlighten my darkness.*

3) Candlestick--a man's place of service

Luke 8:16, *No man, when he hath lighted a candle, covereth it with a vessel, or putteth it under a bed; but setteth it on a candlestick, that they which enter in may see the light.*

E. The lighting of the candle

Matthew 5:15, *Neither do men light a candle, and put it under a bushel, but on a candlestick; and it giveth light unto all that are in the house.*

1) It is a divine work.

II Corinthians 4:6, *For God, who commanded the light to shine out of darkness, hath shined in our hearts, to give the light of the knowledge of the glory of God in the face of Jesus Christ.*

2) It is a separating work.

II Corinthians 6:14, *Be ye not unequally yoked together with unbelievers: for what fellowship hath righteousness with unrighteousness? and what communion hath light with darkness?*

3) It is a personal work to every man.

Ephesians 5:8, *For ye were sometimes darkness, but now are ye light in the Lord: walk as children of light:*

F.   The placing of a candle

Matthew 5:15, *Neither do men light a candle, and put it under a bushel, but on a candlestick; and it giveth light unto all that are in the house.*

1)   Not under a bushel

2)   On a candlestick

3)   Out in the open

G.   The shining of the candle

Matthew 5:16, *Let your light so shine before men, that they may see your good works, and glorify your Father which is in heaven.*

1)   Lightens the darkness

2)   Shines before men

3)   Glorifies our Father in heaven

2.   THE GOOD SAMARITAN

Luke 10:30-35, *And Jesus answering said, A certain man went down from Jerusalem to Jericho, and fell among thieves, which stripped him of his raiment, and wounded him, and departed, leaving him half dead.*
v. 31, *And by chance there came down a certain priest that way: and when he saw him, he passed by on the other side.*
v. 32, *And likewise a Levite, when he was at the place, came and looked on him, and passed by on the other side.*
v. 33, *But a certain Samaritan, as he journeyed, came where he was: and when he saw him, he had compassion on him,*
v. 34, *And went to him, and bound up his wounds, pouring in oil and wine, and set him on his own beast, and brought him to an inn, and took care of him.*
v. 35, *And on the morrow when he departed, he took out two pence, and gave them to the host, and said unto him, Take care of him; and whatsoever thou spendest more, when I come again, I will repay thee.*

A.   Characters involved:

1)   The wounded man was an unknown Jew.

123

2)   The priest and the Levite were religious leaders of Israel.

3)   The Samaritan was the hated enemy of the Jews.

B.   The priest and the Levite were indifferent neighbors.

1)   They neglected to show mercy.

I John 3:17-18, *But whoso hath this world's good, and seeth his brother have need, and shutteth up his bowels of compassion from him, how dwelleth the love of God in him?*
v. 18, *My little children, let us not love in word, neither in tongue; but in deed and in truth.*

2)   They were teachers but not doers of the law.

Romans 2:13, *For not the hearers of the law are just before God, but the doers of the law shall be jsutified.*

James 1:22, *But be ye doers of the word, and not hears only, deceiving your own selves.*

C.   The Samaritan was a good neighbor.

1)   He had compassion on his enemy.

Matthew 5:44, *But I say unto you, Love your enemies, bless them that curse you, do good to them that hate you, and pray for them which despitefully use you, and persecute;*

2)   He ministered unto his needs.

Romans 12:20, *Therefore if thine enemy hunger, feed him; if he thirst, give him drink: for in so doing thou shalt heap coals of fire on his head.*

3)   He went the "second mile."

Matthew 5:41, *. . .whosoever shall compel thee to go a mile, go with him twain.*

D.   The royal law, "love thy neighbor"

   1)   As thyself

   James 2:8, *If ye fulfil the royal law according to the scripture, Thou shalt love thy neighbour as thyself, ye do well:*

   Galatians 5:14, *For all the law is fulfilled in one word, even in this; Thou shalt love thy neighbour as thyself.*

   2)   Without respect of person

   I Timothy 5:21, *I charge thee before God, and the Lord Jesus Christ, and the elect angels, that thou observe these things without preferring one before another, doing nothing by partiality.*

   James 2:1, 9, *My brethren, have not the faith of our Lord Jesus Christ, the Lord of glory, with respect of persons.*

   v. 9, *But if ye have respect to persons, ye commit sin, and are convinced of the law of transgressors.*

   3)   As God loved the world

   John 3:16, *For God so loved the world, that he gave his only begotten Son, that whosoever believeth in him should not perish, but have everlasting life.*

   John 15:12, *This is my commandment, that ye love one another, as I have loved you.*

NOTES

_____

_____

_____

_____

_____

_____

_____

_____

_____

_____

_____

_____

_____

_____

_____

_____

_____

_____

_____

_____

_____

_____

_____

_____

CHRISTIAN FOUNDATIONS

Lesson 22

WHY WE BELIEVE
IN THE HEREAFTER

INTRODUCTION:

The righteous are destined to eternal life in the presence of God. Calvary made it possible. The destiny of the wicked is eternal separation from God that is known as the second death. The God of love will then become a God of justice.

READING:

Revelation 20:10-11, *And the devil that deceived them was cast into the lake of fire and brimstone, where the beast and the false prophet are, and shall be tormented day and night for ever and ever.*
v. 11, *And I saw a great white throne, and him that sat on it, from whose face the earth and the heaven fled away; and there was found no place for them.*

Revelation 21:1-4, *And I saw a new heaven and a new earth: for the first heaven and the first earth were passed away; and there was no more sea.*
v. 2, *And I John saw the holy city, new Jerusalem, coming down from God out of heaven, prepared as a bride adorned for her husband.*
v. 3, *And I heard a great voice out of heaven saying, Behold, the tabernacle of God is with men, and he will dwell with them, and they shall be his people, and God himself shall be with them, and be their God.*
v. 4, *And God shall wipe away all tears from their eyes; and there shall be no more death, death, neither sorrow, nor crying, neither shall there be any more pain: for the former things are passed away.*

1.   THE PROMISE OF CHRIST

A.   Heavenly citizenship to believers

1)   John 14:1-4, *Let not your heart be troubled: ye believe in God, believe also in me.*
v. 2, In my Father's house are many mansions: if it were not so, I would have told you. I go to prepare a place for you.
v. 3, And if I go and prepare a place for you, I will come again, and receive you unto myself; that where I am, there ye may be also.
v. 4, And whither I go ye know, and the way ye know.

2)   Philippians 3:20-21, *For our conversation is in heaven; from whence also we look for the Saviour, the Lord Jesus Christ:*
v. 21, Who shall change our vile body, that it may be fashioned like unto his glorious body, according to the working whereby he is able even to subdue all things unto himself.

B.   Eternal damnation for the wicked

Revelation 20:15, *And whosoever was not found written in the book of life was cast into the lake of fire.*

Revelation 21:8, *But the fearful, and unbelieving, and the abominable, and murderers, and whoremongers, and sorcerers, and idolaters, and all liars, shall have their part in the lake which burneth with fire and brimstone: which is the second death.*

C.   Two resurrections

1)   One will be for the righteous; another will be for the wicked.

John 5:28-29, *Marvel not at this: for the hour is coming, in the which all that are in the graves shall hear his voice,*
v. 29, And shall come forth; they that have done good, unto the resurrection of life; and they that have done evil, unto the resurrection of damnation.

2) They will be separated by 1,000 years.

Revelation 20:4-5, *And I saw thrones, and they sat upon them, and judgment was given unto them: and I saw the souls of them that were beheaded for the witness of Jesus, and for the word of God, and which had not worshipped the beast, neither his image, neither had received his mark upon their foreheads, or in their hands; and they lived and reigned with Christ a thousand years.*
v. 5, But the rest of the dead lived not again until the thousand years were finished. This is the first resurrection.

2. THE TWO JUDGMENTS

A. The judgment of the righteous will be according to their works.

1) II Corinthians 5:10, *For we must all appear before the judgment seat of Christ; that every one may receive the things done in his body, according to that he hath done, whether it be good or bad.*

2) I Corinthians 3:10-15, *According to the grace of God which is given unto me, as a wise masterbuilder, I have laid the foundation, and another buildeth thereon. But let every man take heed how he buildeth thereupon.*
v. 11, For other foundation can no man lay than that is laid, which is Jesus Christ.
v. 12, Now if any man build upon this foundation gold, silver, precious stones, wood, hay, stubble;
v. 13, Every man's work shall be made manifest: for the day shall declare it, because it shall be revealed by fire; and the fire shall try every man's work of what sort it is.
v. 14, If any man's work abide which he hath built thereupon, he shall receive a reward.
v. 15, If any man's work shall be burned, he shall suffer loss: but he himself shall be saved; yet so as by fire.

B. The judgment of the wicked will be at the Great White Throne Judgment.

Revelation 20:11-15, *And I saw a great white throne, and him that sat on it, from whose face the earth and the heaven fled away; and there was found no place for them.*
v. 12, And I saw the dead, small and great, stand before God; and the books were opened: and another book was opened, which is the book of life: and the dead were judged out of those things which were written in the books, according to their works.

v. 13, *And the sea gave up the dead which were in it: and death and hell delivered up the dead which were in them: and they were judged every man according to their works.*
v. 14, *And death and hell were cast into the lake of fire. This is the second death.*
v. 15, *And whosoever was not found written in the book of life was cast into the lake of fire.*

3.   HEAVEN--REWARD OF THE RIGHTEOUS

A.   Christ has promised a heavenly home.

John 14:2, *In my Father's house are many mansions: if it were not so, I would have told you. I go to prepare a place for you.*

B.   We will have fellowship with Christ.

John 14:3, *And if I go and prepare a place for you, I will come again, and receive you unto myself; that where I am, there ye may be also.*

C.   Sorrow and affliction will be banished.

Revelation 21:4, *And God shall wipe away all tears from their eyes; and there shall be no more death, neither sorrow, nor crying, neither shall there be any more pain: for the former things are passed away.*

D.   Death will be vanquished forever.

Revelation 21:4, *. . .there shall be no more death. . .*

4.   HELL--REWARD OF THE WICKED

A.   The wicked will be cast into everlasting fire.

Revelation 20:14-15, *And death and hell were cast into the lake of fire. This is the second death.*
v. 15, *And whosoever was not found written in the book of life was cast into the lake of fire.*

B.   They will have vile companionship for eternity.

Revelation 21:8, *But the fearful, and unbelieving, and the abominable, and murderers, and whoremongers, and sorcerers, and idolaters, and all liars, shall have their part in the lake which burneth with fire and brimstone: which is the second death.*

C.   They will be haunted by memory and remorse.

Luke 16:19-31, *There was a certain rich man, which was clothed in purple and fine linen, and fared sumptuously every day:*
v. 20, *And there was a certain beggar named Lazarus, which was laid at his gate, full of sores,*
v. 21, *And desiring to be fed with the crumbs which fell from the rich man's table: moreover the dogs came and licked his sores.*
v. 22, *And it came to pass, that the beggar died, and was carried by the angels into Abraham's bosom: the rich man also died, and was buried;*
v. 23, *And in hell he lift up his eyes, being in torments, and seeth Abraham afar off, and Lazarus in his bosom.*
v. 24, *And he cried and said, Father Abraham, have mercy on me, and send Lazarus, that he may dip the tip of his finger in water, and cool my tongue; for I am tormented in this flame.*
v. 25, *But Abraham said, Son, remember that thou in thy lifetime receivedst thy good things, and likewise Lazarus evil things: but now he is comforted, and thou art tormented.*
v. 26, *And beside all this, between us and you there is a great gulf fixed: so that they which would pass from hence to you cannot; neither can they pass to us, that would come from thence.*
v. 27, *Then he said, I pray thee therefore, father, that thou wouldest send him to my father's house:*
v. 28, *For I have five brethren; that he may testify unto them, lest they also come into this place of torment.*
v. 29, *Abraham saith unto him, They have Moses and the prophets; let them hear them.*
v. 30, *And he said, Nay, father Abraham: but if one went unto them from the dead, they will repent.*
v. 31, *And he said unto him, If they hear not Moses and the prophets, neither will they be persuaded, though one rose from the dead.*

D.   Hell is the final separation from God.

Luke 16:26, *. . .between us and you there is a great gulf fixed: so that they which would pass from hence to you cannot; neither can they pass to us, that would come from thence.*

5.   FALSE VIEWS

A.   Universalism teaches that everyone finally will be saved, that God is too loving to exclude anyone from heaven. Scripture disputes this.

John 3:18, 36, *He that believeth on him is not condemned: but he that believeth not is condemned already, because he hath not believed in the name of the only begotten Son of God.*

v. 36, *He that believeth on the Son hath everlasting life: and he that believeth not the Son shall not see life; but the wrath of God abideth on him.*

B.   Restorationism teaches that punishment in hell is not eternal but a temporary experience for the purpose of purifying the sinner to fit him for heaven.

Revelation 20:14, *. . .death and hell were cast into the lake of fire. . .the second death.*

C.   Second Probationism teaches that all will have a second chance to accept salvation between death and resurrection. The scriptures teach that at death man's destiny is fixed.

Hebrews 9:27, *And as it is appointed unto men once to die, but after this the judgment:*

D.   Annihilationism teaches that God will annihilate the wicked. They use the scriptures which set forth death as the penalty for sin, but in these cases, the reference to spiritual death means separation from God.

Romans 6:23, *For the wages of sin is death; but the gift of God is eternal life through Jesus Christ our Lord.*

CONCLUSION:

Man was given the privilege of choosing his destiny. His present decisions will forever seal this destiny. As creatures of choice, let us make our spiritual investments sure--all for Christ!